The Way We Are

The Way We Are

BY

Allen Wheelis

W. W. Norton & Company

NEW YORK   LONDON

For information about permission to reproduce selections from this book,
write to Permissions, W. W. Norton & Company, Inc., 500 Fifth Avenue,
New York, NY 10110

Manufacturing by Courier Westford
Book design by Brooke Koven
Production manager: Julia Druskin

Library of Congress Cataloging-in-Publication Data

Wheelis, Allen, 1915–
The way we are / by Allen Wheelis.— 1st ed.
p. cm.
Includes bibliographical references.
ISBN-13: 978-0-393-06214-4 (hardcover)
ISBN-10: 0-393-06214-7 (hardcover)
1. Psychology. I. Title.
BF121.W463 2006
150—dc22

2006002294

W. W. Norton & Company, Inc.
500 Fifth Avenue, New York, N.Y. 10110
www.wwnorton.com

W. W. Norton & Company Ltd.
Castle House, 75/76 Wells Street, London W1T 3QT

1 2 3 4 5 6 7 8 9 0

for Joan

CONTENTS

Introduction 15

WAYS OF POWER

I *The Nature of Man* 23
II *Groups* 37
III *The Scheme of Things* 41
IV *Power* 53
V *Sovereignty* 79

WAYS OF THE HEART

VI *Desire* 95
VII *Fidelity* 107
VIII *Loss* 123
IX *Love* 131

Acknowledgments 143

The Way We Are

Where are you, friend to whom
I could tell the truth
without plunging you into despair?
                                    —ELIAS CANETTI

INTRODUCTION

In a maze and lost, we follow now this lead, now another, veer this way and that through corridors of anguish, boredom, and—oh, so rarely!—joy. What are we up to? Where are we going? To what purpose? Occasionally we glimpse a phantom vision, gone in a flicker. We search for an informing principle, a truth that will teach us how to live, will define our task, enable us to transcend our folly and cruelty, to use ourselves up in a way that counts.

The way to live should issue from our nature, from what it is we believe ourselves most deeply to be. We tend to assume that we know what we are, that our nature is obvious, given to us by direct observation of others and of ourselves: Just look around the world and look into your own heart and you will know the human condition. It's not so. What it is to be a human being is not clear at all, but deeply shrouded. Because, in the evolution from animal life to human life, along with the gain in knowledge and awareness, we have gained also the ability to deceive ourselves. We arrange *not to know* our nature, *not to see* what we are up to. Our self-deceptions are so dense, piled on so thick, like layers of paint on a canvas already painted, layer after layer, laid on from school and pulpit and lectern and TV and Internet, that it is all but impossible to break through, to get a clear view of what we really are.

Behind our loudly professed values of freedom, justice, and equality lies a propensity to violence far stronger and far deeper than is known to any of us, even the most cynical. It is all but invincible, invades even the bedroom, corrupts what we call love. We indulge in vast hypocrisies, flagrant and subtle, to conceal from ourselves this destructiveness. We are in fact largely the opposite of what we think we are.

And as we deceive ourselves, we deceive also others. Self-awareness comes into being in the midst of struggles for power and is immediately put to use. One defends oneself, or seeks advantage, by misrepresenting oneself. One doesn't think about it; it happens instantly, automatically, inalienably. It is not possible to abstain. One cannot be oneself. To be human is to be false. Awareness is inseparable from misrepresentation. The soul of self-awareness is deception.

Revealing myself, I remain hidden. As the real self is exposed, it becomes false, the now-real self retreating in shadow behind the newly false. Honesty cannot know itself; aware of telling the truth, I lie. The pure heart, blind to its own purity, sees only outward; the reflective heart is devious. Unaware of weeping, I show you a moment of authentic grief; be quick, it's gone in a flash. As I feel the tears on my face, knowing how they may alter *your* reaction, grief is mediated, is being staged. I am brokenhearted. Truly. Truly? Yes, but am making sure that you know it—while arranging somehow not myself to know I'm doing it. The reality to which that "truly" refers is a slippery item. "Say everything that comes to mind," the analyst says to the analysand, "nothing must remain hidden"; but the first association scurries for cover as the second is being staged by the third, and the bottom of that barrel can never be scraped. Below the deepest uncovering one yet deeper is possible. Dirt is endless. Fur and feces and bones, and ever deeper, but no bedrock. Authenticity is fugitive in self-referential systems; awareness builds layer by layer while reality flees forward.

I must take myself as an object of study, must use my friends and my patients only as checks and limits. He who studies others will find much of interest but not the human condition. The most important things about human life we come upon from within and can know only from within.

I am obsessed with death; and this obsession, I am convinced, is not a private terror but the unchanging backdrop to the stage of our existence. We block it from view with contrived sets that we call reality, and though we know those sets to be fake we labor endlessly to make them look real. And as we go about those actions on that stage which accord with those sets, we come finally to believe they *are* real. The backdrop behind them is forgotten.

These are the two essential categories: that unchanging backdrop, the raw nature of existence, unadorned, unmediated, overwhelming us with dread, *the way things are*; and that changing succession of stage sets which we put up in front of the backdrop, blocking it from view, *the schemes of things,* the systems of meanings within which we live. The backdrop is a constant, too awful and too fearful to be endured; the sets change over the course of history, though they may seem fixed over the course of a lifetime. The set, as in a play, is the arrangement in which we live, the scheme of things.

Psychoanalysis attends to those distortions of mind that have come about as a result of mishap and mistreatment in childhood. It attempts the correction of these distortions by means of understanding. Not just analysts and analysands, but all of us, simply by being members of a culture permeated with the promise of psychology, share in the belief that such is possible. And as we, acting on this belief, go about the process of analyzing the miseries visited upon us by the preceding generation, it comes insidiously to seem that all misery is of this kind, not destiny but mishap, that therefore if people generally were free of neuroses we would no longer torment ourselves and our families, nor would tyrants torment their subjects (nor themselves even want to be tyrants), and that human life would then be happy and secure. Thus psychology slides into place as the modern ideology, the heir to religion. It is the scheme of things in which we live.

None of this, however, is of concern to me. The subject of my inquiry lies beyond psychology. It is the human condition itself. I want to know what is possible for man and what is precluded to man on the basis of that psychology which must be ascribed to him in order for him to be a man at all. Not the misery consequent to chance and mistreatment, which in principle may be remediable, but the misery that would remain, irremediable, simply by virtue of being a human being. That is my subject. What is the minimum penalty for being a conscious and self-conscious creature living simultaneously in an eternal

symbolic world of our own construction and in the nat‐
ural world in which, looking straight ahead, we see our
oncoming death? Indeed, what suffering that we might
wish to consider as avoidable or treatable must we con‐
clude issues, not from mistreatment, but from this condi‐
tion? And, further, what portion of that mistreatment of
man by man and of child by parent, all of which appears
gratuitous, may prove to be the unavoidable outcome of
conditions that define the human state itself?

All of the themes of my life are here drawn together and
reexamined, and passages appear here that have appeared
in earlier books of mine. Too late perhaps to come upon
a new vision, but still possible perhaps to set forth—with
greater clarity, concision, and bluntness—what I know of
the ways of power and the ways of the heart.

WAYS OF POWER

I

The Nature of Man

Only the first life fed on nonlife. Thereafter life feeds on life. Big fish eat little fish. Jaws develop fangs. Hawk falls on hare, bird takes worm; wings flutter in the teeth of the fox. Man eats hare, fish, fowl, lamb.

We are both predator and victim. We kill those who have more to eat than we, or who threaten to take what we have—or who do not threaten but whom we so imagine.

We kill to take the female or the territory of a rival. A rival is one who has a female or a territory we desire.

Property is a function of the willingness to fight. Titles are written in blood. Dusty deeds rest on old murders.

We are children of slime, our teeth break bone, suck marrow, we live on others; we devour their lives without ever seeing their faces. The magic of money and commerce keeps them far away, their screams unheard.

Everyone eats but few kill. Technicians fell the lamb. Eating becomes a ceremony of innocence, tinkle of crystal, rustle of taffeta. Teeth are for beauty: straighten them, make them whiter, the smile more loving. Visit every restaurant in town, never pass the house of slaughter.

Leather shoes and belt, mink coat, alligator handbag, gloves of calf, lizard watchbands, peacock feathers—how we deck ourselves in the skins and scraps—yet never strike a blow, never cut a throat. We push away our own destructiveness, make it alien, become finally unaware, see only the destructiveness of others.

The tendency of civilization is not to eliminate destructiveness, nor even to diminish it, but to remove it. Tooth to hand to stone to blade to bullet to bomb—so man estranges himself from his victim. Our fate falls now from the touch of a finger in an underground bunker half a world away.

Those who create the images we think we live by stand most aloof from the destructiveness by which, equally, we live. Poet and philosopher sit to meat, speak of love, charity, rights of man, sacredness of life. Far away blood flows, cries rise in the night. We benefit from such order as our cities afford, but it's the cop on the beat who pistol-whips the thug. We are beneficiaries of the affluent society—the museums, universities, theaters, libraries—of an armed and sovereign state; but it's the soldier who fights the wars which that state, however mistakenly, considers necessary for its survival.

So it comes about that those who teach us what life is, or should be, who create our image of ourselves, find killing to be ugly, mean, and set about in their dismay to draw maps of human nature in which destruction has no primary place, to make songs, poems, world views, religions, which portray killing as unnecessary, a kind of waywardness or error into which we have fallen, from which, by these creations of theirs, we must be rescued. Such maps become new justifications for more extensive killings. Holocausts are in the name of peace, freedom, justice, truth.

We kill men who threaten our holy faiths—Sun God, Christ, white skin, free enterprise—or who do not threaten but whom we choose so to construe.

The anguish of the Circus Maximus reappears at but a greater distance in the Last Judgment. It reappears quite immediately—with a violence greater by far than that of the Circus—in the Holy Inquisition and the Thirty Years War.

We destroy and we create. Without destruction there is no creation. Let those who praise life know that they praise equally the destroying and the creating. Monuments of murder and spires of devotion rise side by side, reach up to heaven.

We come now to a time when our capacity to tear down dazzles our capacity to build.

Conscience is the mandate of the group installed in one beating heart, enforces murder and brotherhood with equal authority.

Hydrogen warheads sleep lightly in underground nests.

Evil flickers here, there, everywhere, a wildfire out of control. Put it out here, it flares there. Everywhere. It is also inside ourselves, has crept into the deepest reaches of our heart. There is no good man. We all are killers, we live on others. And when, rarely, we can bring ourselves to admit it, we say ruefully, piously, "Christ was right, we *all* are fallen, we *all* are sinners."

Fallen? From what? Where was that state of grace from which we are supposed to have fallen?

The innocence we ascribe to the childhood of humanity is the innocence we have come to know only much later, east of Eden, the innocence possible to us within the knowledge of good and evil. Such innocence consists in following the rules that banish violence. Therefore, as we project such obedience backward, we picture a gentle Eden wherein the lion and the lamb lie down together. And right there we've got it dead wrong. The innocence of our prehistory, our Garden of Eden, is the innocence of unlimited violence, of acting according to nature. There were then no taboos to set limits, hence no good and no evil.

The boundary zone of our existence is a forbidden territory called the sacred. We know we are there by signs. Voices are lowered and hushed, we tread softly, look up respectfully, apprehensively. We are warned to keep away. Near the boundary itself we are taken over by fear and trembling. We are too close to God. Common sense tugs at our sleeve: Turn back! Beyond the limit is great power. Those who cross that limit are struck down. Some few, able to seize and control the thunderbolts, become gods.

The sacred is a minefield barring the way back. It lies

between us and the freedom we have lost, the violence we so fear and so desire, the rush, the oneness of life, the fusion, the continuity, the not-knowing. The approach is posted with taboos. Gods patrol the border ceaselessly, drive us onward, warn us not to look back. We can never go home again. Nor can we ever forget or stop longing.

Before mankind was enlightened, the awful power beyond the *natural* limits, securely removed from the ability of man to reach or control or to manipulate, was invoked by our priests and medicine men to strengthen those *moral* and *sexual* limits that man, by his own will, is capable of violating. The giant lurking in the earth who shakes our house down, he or some other giant just like him, we are told, patrols also the sexual and moral boundaries. Watch out! God is everywhere. If you transgress He will punish you.

Now we are enlightened; and enlightenment, it transpires, draws in its train strange, perhaps sinister, implications. After the initial grand victories of reason come disturbing aftershocks. *Natural* limits have been divested of meaning. If famine sweeps the land, that's bad luck, but it is not God punishing us or telling us something. It's but the impersonal, meaningless operation of natural forces.

The awful and the terrifying beyond the natural limits, therefore, cannot be used to maintain the inviolability of *moral* and *sexual* limits. No longer can we lend to morality the authority of lightning, of earthquake, of tidal wave. The Enlightenment has washed us up on an alien shore: *All of our limits are variables,* all are within our control. We may draw them in closer or push them out farther. There is no God to establish any position; so every position is arbitrary. If we wish to designate something as sacred and inviolate, we are free do to so, and others are equally free to spit on it. If we wish to exterminate all the Jews . . . well, no big deal. It requires only systematic propaganda, an efficient bureaucracy, a well-developed heavy industry, and soon the transports will be rolling. If we wish to kill all of the people of Dresden . . . no need to go to Washington for that, or even to London; the decision can be taken at the Air Command Center.

And why not? With no authority beyond humanity, by what standard can we designate anything as absolutely wrong? Wrong beyond reach of reconsideration? Whatever the nature of the limit, beyond that limit lies power. And that further increment of power will increase the temptation to yet further violation for a yet further augmentation of power.

Free to choose how to live, the way we choose is meaningless; living in the certainty of meaning, we live a life that is imposed.

How did we arrive at such a condition? Try to imagine it. Look back. Reach far back to our remote past. Look! A green savannah, tall grass sways in the wind like waves of the sea. An occasional tree. It is a vast plain, vast as if endless, stretching to the horizon, on to the next horizon, and on farther, thousands of miles across what now is northern Africa and India. Peaceful, quiet, fertile. Then we hear a chattering. We see *them*—small, apelike creatures, our animal forebears; and, seeing them, we see ourselves in an earlier condition. This is perhaps the first picture in our family album.

Now conjure a scene in the same place, a few million years later, now Egypt of the Fourth Dynasty. Here we see the descendants of those apelike creatures, our more recent forebears, quite human now, lifting heavy stones, placing them one upon another. Tens of thousands labor endlessly under the weight of those stones.

The creatures in the first scene live in a state of nature; the creatures of the second in a state of civilization. What has happened? What are the features of that fateful movement?

As proto-human beings begin using tools, they become aware that a goal that cannot be reached immediately can be reached indirectly, through a series of related steps. Consciousness, formerly limited to ends, now begins to include means; and these means make it possible to pur-

sue more distant ends. Tools fall together into combina-
tions, and thereby multiply. The proliferation of tools
enlarges the scope of what can be accomplished with
them, which in turn enlarges the consciousness that now
can visualize ever more distant ends.

In animals, fear is episodic; in humans, because of their
enlarged consciousness, fear is constant. Even in our
pleasures, our triumphs, fear is a lurking presence. We are
never safe. We live in vivid awareness of dangers not present but remembered or anticipated—drought and famine
and predators, pain and pestilence and war. And something new: the awareness that we will die.

Constant fear gives birth to exploitation. Because we
are afraid we seek refuge in strength. We create gods to
protect us, to explain our condition, to guarantee our
safety, to promise us eternal life. And these gods, it turns
out, speak to us through men of power—through wiz-
ards, priests, princes, prelates, and kings. They formulate
the taboos: impulse must be controlled, violence and random sexuality prohibited. Sin comes into being. And
morality. And guilt, the danger from within. Heaven is
created for those who observe the taboos, hell for those
who violate them. Fear and weakness impel us to honor
the taboos, to obey our leaders. It is now possible for the
few to control the many. Work comes into being: steady,
heavy labor day after day for an end which is not of our
choosing, which serves no purpose in our life but which
(we have been convinced) is required by the gods who

(we have come to believe) will protect us. Servitude is invented.

The proliferation of tools and of the things that are built with tools, and the proliferation of myths and of the fears that are formulated and expressed by myths, comprise culture. Henceforth man lives, not in nature, but in culture.

In our nostalgia for the major freedoms of animal life we remember a Golden Age, a Garden, a time before sin. The sacred does not beckon to us from up ahead, urging us forward toward higher spiritual realms. The sacred lies behind us. It blocks the way back to the freedom of our prehuman past. The sacred and the forbidden are one.

Consider once more the animals of the first scene. Their sexuality is our sexuality, their aggression is our aggression. The motives that drive them as they hunt and kill and copulate also drive us. But look! When the weather is mild and they have had their fill of food and of sex they take their ease. They sleep and play and disport themselves. They do not make monuments. And regard once more the multitude under the weight of those stones. They have no time to play, to disport themselves. The tombs of their gods reach into the sky.

The animals live in a group of about thirty or thirty-five. It does not get much larger. The naturally given qualities of leadership and social cohesion cannot organize a greater number. When it gets larger, it splits. But in building the pyramids the group is in the thousands. Tens of thousands. We cannot even begin to count them. How is this possible? How is it that so many, engaged in such punitive labor, can yet form a stable group? It's true there are a few guards about. A few supervisors, perhaps. But clearly there does not exist here sufficient force to keep these men working. A very few of these workers could kill all of the guards. So why don't they? Why do they continue, meekly, in this onerous task? Why don't they rebel?

Because Eden lies behind them, and the way back is blocked. These men live in the knowledge of good and evil. They have given up random violence and indiscriminate sexuality. And from that abnegation arises all of the human virtues: faithfulness, honesty, charity, obedience, love, trust, and care. It is these virtues that make it possible that orderly organized life can now take place in groups—not of thirty or thirty-five—but of thousands. Hundreds of thousands.

Millions of people observe the taboos and live orderly law-abiding lives within one organized group. The orderliness, indeed, is breathtaking. Regard Park Avenue at rush hour. Three lanes of taxis fleeing north, three lanes rushing south. Thousands and thousands of vehicles all moving at about thirty miles per hour. Presently the lights turn red, and all stop at the same moment. Now, on the odd numbered cross-streets, single lines of cars flee across Park Avenue to the west, while on the even numbered streets single lines rush toward the East River. Regard the freeways near the Los Angeles Airport; the sky festooned with concrete ribbons streaking up and around, under and over, layer upon layer, curving like rainbows, along which speed thousands and thousands of cars.

It is the morality of individuals that makes possible the orderly life of aggregates.

There is, however, a hook attached to this remarkable progression from animal to man, and we should—in the midst of our self-congratulation—have a look at it.

The violence that individuals have given up in the course of becoming orderly and moral has not been eliminated. It is passed on; it is handed upward. It collects at the top, in the White House, Number Ten Downing Street, the Reichstag, the Kremlin. The morality of individuals has led to community, to group solidarity, to orderliness, thereby making possible larger and larger sovereign collectives. And these collectives seize for themselves all of that power, all of that ruthlessness, that savagery, that the constituent individuals have, in their move to morality, to decency, themselves forsworn. These sovereign entities, however, have forsworn nothing, have not themselves become moral. Such was never their intention, though they are loud in lip service to that notion. And the savagery that these collectives, these super-beasts in their super-jungle, are able to inflict on each other and on their moral constituents is so much more destructive than anything that could be done by individuals—regard the German dead at the Falaise Gap, thousands and thousands of bodies, heads, limbs, viscera; the beach at Iwo Jima after the battle, nothing moving amid all those dead but the remorseless and now-red tide; Stalingrad at night, the frozen bodies in the empty silent streets, everything still except for the rustle of rats; the vast armada of planes over Berlin, the relentless thunder of bombs, the endless explosions, fires; the boiling cloud over Hiroshima stretching slowly up, up, up, reaching finally six miles into the clear early morning sky—so much more destructive than anything that could possibly be done by individuals, that we may permit ourselves some nostalgia for the untrammeled violence of our pre-human past.

II

Groups

The group is primary. The noble savage, should ever we find him, has already been shaped by the savage group from which he came. The outlaw is outside the law but still within the group, pursues his life of solitary crime only with the support of the sustaining, complexly interrelated activities of the despised community around him—depending on Detroit for his getaway car, on Chevron for the gas, on Smith and Wesson for his gun, on McDonald's for his forlorn hamburger.

As a viable social arrangement, anarchy is but a dream of the disaffected.

We as individuals, therefore, must concern ourselves with the survival and welfare of the group as well as the pursuit of personal security and happiness.

All groups make rules that limit individual behavior. These limitations are deemed necessary by the group to secure its survival. That survival then depends on the ability of the group to enforce its rules. So begins morality.

The individual lives within many groups, and the morality issuing from the observance of one set of rules, may differ from, and conflict with, the morality generated by another. Planned Parenthood and Right to Life contend with each other; both have their moral heroes, both mourn their martyrs.

The authority of groups is hierarchical; the last word belongs to the group that has the authority to lock you up and to kill you, and, likewise, the authority to put you in uniform and send you forth to kill others.

The rules of the sovereign state take precedence over the rules of any subordinate group within the state, and take precedence likewise over the rules of any larger and more inclusive group beyond the state, such as the United Nations, the Catholic Church, Amnesty International, the World Court.

The rules that determine right and wrong, therefore, are made, not by the most inclusive group, nor by the wisest, nor by the one best qualified to judge such matters, but by the strongest.

The rules that shape our lives defend the interests of the holders of power.

In matters of conscience, warriors instruct priests.

The draft resister claims a higher authority, but the state sends him to jail.

III

The Scheme of
Things

Animals live within the limits of their lives as bio-
logically given, within circumstances that are
environmentally given. There is no separation of
self from environment, therefore no sense of self. There is
no knowledge of death, no watching of one's fateful progression, no history, no vision of one's actual condition,
hence no need to transcend that condition. Needs are
immediate; when they are met the animal is content.
There are no transcendent needs.

The moment approaches. Perhaps a million years in
duration, still but a moment in the long journey. Con-

sciousness enlarges to include one's oncoming and inevitable death. One becomes aware of one's self as distinct from one's surroundings, knows one's actual condition, moving through time, growing older, doomed. The animal is becoming human. This is the Fall. Culture is about to begin.

The immediate horror man perceives is his own death, but beyond that he begins to see the entire life process as carnage, as eating and being eaten. A terrible screaming pervades the universe. Man is the first to hear it. This is the vision we cannot accept. It drives toward madness or despair.

What does Christianity do with this vision? It does not deny it; it makes it acceptable. What Christianity does for the true believer is give him strength to bear it. Redeems it. That's the word! The scheme of things *redeems* the way things are.

But what is redemption? It must be an interpretation. The scheme of things interprets the way things are as necessary to something grand. The scheme of things, therefore, is both a diagram of the something grand and an interpretation of the way things are as an essential step on the way to the something grand. The life process thereupon becomes less horrible and more bearable because it serves, however obscurely, a glorious end. One's

individual life is redeemed when it is in the service of the
something grand.

The beginning of the redemption of life is the beginning of culture. All culture is redemption. The history of
culture is the history of the changing forms by which a
short and brutish life has been redeemed. The culture of
a people, writes T. S. Eliot, is the incarnation of its religion. "Any religion, while it lasts, provides the framework
for a culture, and protects the mass of humanity from
boredom and despair."

Man searches for a scheme of things larger than his own
life, with greater authority, to which he may belong. The
hunger from which this search issues is profound and
inalienable. If he can find such a scheme and make his life
"mean" something in it, that is, contribute to it, make a
difference, he will have ferried something of his mortal
self across the gulf of death to become a part of something that will live on. The doomed life must leave a
residue of value. The carrier and guarantor of this value is
a man-made scheme of things perceived as reality and
presumed to be eternal.

What can one say of the way things are? That the con-
structions of mind are not coextensive with existence,

that there is something "out there," a universe independent of man, there before we arrived and to be there after we have disappeared. It affects us and we it. It and we are in continual contact and interaction, and we know it not. We cannot bear to know. An angel, detached and immortal, could know; we, mired in mortality, are at risk. Interest deflects our knowing. Our lives depend on its being other than it is. In the midst of the way things are we know only the scheme of things in which we live.

The scheme of things is a system of order. Beginning as our view of the world, it finally *becomes* our world. We live within the space defined by its coordinates. It is self-evidently true, is accepted so naturally and automatically that one is not aware of an act of acceptance having taken place. It comes with our mother's milk, is chanted in school, proclaimed from the White House, insinuated by television, validated at Harvard. Like the air we breathe, the scheme of things disappears, becomes simply reality, becomes, as far as we can tell, the way things are. *It is the lie necessary to life.* The world as it exists beyond that scheme becomes vague, irrelevant, largely unperceived, finally nonexistent.

As soon as the scheme of things is questioned, it has lost its capacity to redeem. "What, then," Camus writes, "is that incalculable feeling that deprives the mind of the sleep necessary to life? A world that can be explained even with bad reasons is a familiar world. But . . . in a universe suddenly divested of illusions and lights, man feels an alien, a stranger."

As man emerged from the condition of animal, there must have been a period of transition during which the carriers of the process could not have known what was happening to them or even that a change was taking place. Now in retrospect we can see it as an expansion of awareness which brought into being freedom and choice. The knowing mind begins to know itself and to perceive, along with the freedom to do this or that, a horror about which it has no freedom at all. As soon as we become able, floating down the river of life, really to see the remarkable scenery and to enjoy the newly acquired freedom to move this way or that in the current, at just that moment we hear the roar of the cataract ahead. This is the human condition. Amid the luscious fruits we see the coiled asp. We become, at one stroke, gods and food for worms.

Changes that come about glacially in the transformation of species are reenacted in a flash in the lives of individuals. Thus we may catch a glimpse, each in his own past, of that moment which recapitulates the birth of man, the beginning of that exaltation and anguish which has become for us the condition of life, the air we breathe.

I remember a spring night in a school auditorium, during the rehearsal of a play. I am thirteen. I am weary of the farce, weary of the silliness of the cast, of our endless horseplay, mindlessness. A scene in which I have no part is being rehearsed; I stand in an open door at the rear of the dark and empty hall. A storm is under way. The door is on the lee of the building, and I step out under the overhang. The rain swirls and beats. Lightning reveals a familiar schoolyard in a ghostly light. I feel a sudden poignancy. Images strike my mind. The wind is the scream of a lost spirit, searching the earth and finding no good, recalling old bereavements, lashing the land with tears. Consciousness leaves my body, moves out in time and space. I undergo an expanding awareness of self, of separateness, of time flowing through me, bearing me on, knowing I have a chance, the one chance all of us have, the chance of a life, knowing a time will come when nothing lies ahead and everything lies behind, and hoping I can then look back and feel it well spent. How, in the light of fixed stars, should one live?

So begins the hunger for meaning.

Is the scheme of things the creation of one man? a charismatic leader who achieves a new vision of life and secures a following? Did Christ invent Christianity? I think not. He created disorder, led a rabble, was an irritant to existing schemes of things. The scheme of things which is Christianity, of which his teachings are the nucleus, was the creation of many people over a span much longer than his life. Indeed, by the time it could have been called Christianity it had taken on a character he would have repudiated.

A scheme of things is a social creation, something offered to the individual by society as a system of significance. One's ambition may be secret, but the pattern of meanings that makes possible the ambition and within which it may be realized is social. Even if one's entire hope of meaning in life hinges on acquiring a complete set of American stamps, that vision still is social, depends upon others being similarly engaged; for such an endeavor could mean nothing in a world without stamp collecting.

When a society offers at its apex a scheme of things, inclusive and integrative of all subordinate orientations, and when that scheme by virtue of being generally accepted as true holds great authority, then that society is unified and cohesive, is an organism. Every leader seeks to embody such a scheme of things, and charismatically to make it ever more powerfully appealing, binding on the loyalties of all. When society offers, at the top, contending schemes, none of compelling authority, that society is fragmented.

Should ever any scheme of things acquire absolute authority it would exclude from awareness anything beyond its limits. Nothing then could contend with it and no change could occur. It and the society it organized would be static and immortal. Each individual by allegiance to that scheme would share in that immortality. The dread of death would be overcome.

No scheme of things has ever achieved such authority, though some schemes have endured for millennia. Change is unstoppable; for no scheme of things has ever convinced everyone. All schemes involve limitation and denial. They are man-made. They reach out into the way things are, the realm of the existing, and make order. Then claim to be eternal.

A scheme of things is a plan for salvation. How well it works will depend upon its scope and authority. If it is small, even great achievement in its service will do little to dispel death. We seek the largest possible scheme, not in a hunger for truth, but in a hunger for meaning. The more comprehensive the scheme, the greater its promise of banishing dread. If we can make our lives mean something in a cosmic scheme we will live in the certainty of immortality. The very great success of Christianity for a thousand years follows upon its having been of universal scope, including and accounting for everything, assigning to all things a proper place; offering to every man, whether prince or beggar, savant or fool, the privilege of working in the Lord's vineyard; and upon its being accepted as true throughout the Western world.

As a ruling scheme of things is modified by inroads from outlying existence, it loses authority, is less able to banish dread; its adherents fall away. Eventually it fades, exists only in history, becomes quaint or primitive, becomes, finally, a myth. Our myths were once blueprints of reality. The Church, as defender of the regnant scheme of things, was right to stop Galileo; activities such as his import into the social order new orientations which will eventually destroy that order.

When the ruling scheme of things comes to seem untrue or unimportant, one's efforts within it become meaning-less. One's whole life becomes meaningless. The Heavenly City falls into ruins. The avenue to immortality ends on an abyss. One is cast back on his individual life, stares ahead through a transparence of days to death, which stands at the end. One enters a state of dread.

Life then is borne forward on waves of cynicism and

despair. One seeks distraction, death-defying games per-haps which invoke the specter from which one flinches. By surviving the heightened risk one may achieve briefly the illusion of mastery. But not for long. Within the con-fines of a single life death is unmasterable.

Sometimes the distraction is less desperate and may contain creative possibilities. What began as a distraction from the loss of meaning and the dread of death may come itself to have meaning and to protect against dread. The distraction, that is, becomes a new scheme of things. A committed chess player may finally lose awareness that life contains anything other than chess. A new defense against the Ruy Lopez may be monument enough.

In such a recovery one may move to a scheme of things larger than the one that has crumbled; the crum-bling itself may then be seen in a perspective that makes it meaningful, perhaps even inevitable. So the Marxists of the thirties become the Freudians of the forties, and pol-itics is subsumed under psychology. A. A. Brill was able to comprehend the rash of strikes during the Depression as rebellious sons acting out their defiance of fathers.

For a thousand years Christianity was for the Western world the scheme of things organizing man's worldview. It stood at the apex of a hierarchy within which were included all other schemes, fraternal, artistic, scholastic, political. That world order is now irretrievably lost.

I come back to Eliot's dictum that culture is the incarnation of religion. If that is true—and I believe it's true—a culture cannot forever survive the loss of its religion; for the lesser schemes of things which that culture will still be able to offer will, whatever their merits, lack that element of the sacred which previously had derived from religion, and without which no one of the lesser schemes will be able to achieve the unification of the whole.

Science, like religion, is a scheme of things hierarchically ordered, including many subordinate schemes. The compelling paradigm of one age may, like phlogiston, be but a quaint superstition for the next, without disturbing the overriding rational-scientific scheme of things of which the varying paradigms are subordinate schemes. But science has never, not even in its greatest ascendancy, claimed such cosmic scope as Christianity. Some of the joys and sorrows of man's condition have not, within science, found a place or an accounting. Most particularly now do they find no place; for the rational-scientific scheme of things is itself on the decline. Fewer people now see it as coextensive with reality. More and more frequently people look away from science, or around its edges, in search of some new vision, some new scheme of things with which to order their lives.

IV

Power

The will to power is that quality of a living thing that leads it to grab hold of its environment, to take in what nourishes it, as much as it can, to shoulder aside whoever is interested in the same thing, to trample whatever stands in its way, to grow, to become big and strong, and to multiply. There is no moderation; nothing is too much. The aim of the maggot is to make more maggots, to transform the entire universe into maggots. The drive is blind, knows no internal limit, will continue until stopped.

For most of the duration of life on earth, power was the ability to rend, to tear, to seize, to pin down, to destroy, to gobble up. Significant power in human affairs now, in essence unchanged, is in the form of money, property, position, acclaim, possessions, influence.

The guises of power are so various, so dissembled, that power ceases to be recognized as such. We would have it that human life is discontinuous with life in the tide pools, in the jungle, that mind or spirit, something far removed from power, has come to be the essence of human life. We delude ourselves. The holders of great power may be physically frail, gentle in manner, tender in sentiment, Christian by profession, may wear but a loincloth; but power is power, and its nature is to grab hold, to seize possession, to overwhelm. Whatever appears in human life that seems unrelated to power, or even—like love, like charity, like self-sacrifice—contrary to it, is, if it endures, but another mask of power.

Observe the single free-floating cell. It moves about, this way and that, exploring, seeking. What does it want? It wants to seize the nutrient environment, take it in, grow bigger, stronger. It has heard God's voice: Be fruitful and multiply.

It comes about in time, in our remote evolutionary past, that a number of such cells associate themselves into a community. Something new. Are not these several cells hampered in their competition with other cells by virtue of, as it were, holding hands? Why, yes, very likely. And whenever so hampered, they perish. But it comes about eventually, by chance, that some such association is not hampered but advantaged, finds itself the possessor of superior strength, greater than the summation of its constituent strengths, whereupon the association endures. The will to power of the individual cell is surrendered to the whole. The will of the individual cell comes to be not power but cooperation, faithful service in its subordinate place and function in the life of the organism. It has become servant to the will to power of the whole.

To gain power is to gain respect; it is also—equally, inevitably—to be hated. He who is afraid to be hated is handicapped in his pursuit of power, for with each gain in power will come an increase in hatred. The greater the fear of this hatred, the greater the obstacle to the pursuit of power. One continues on a course of increasing power until fear calls a halt.

Prudence requires that our hatred of the powerful be hidden, while our respect is manifest, often ostentatious. As every king must know, however, the hatred, though invisible, is always present. Uneasy lies the head . . . etc.

Naked power is quicksilver, lost in a flash—a bank robber on the run, hand on his gun, shot down at the next corner. So power rushes to form, which endows power with legitimacy, defines the processes whereby it is acquired, exercised, delegated, transferred. Hiding behind form, power acquires stability. Form is a structure of power but claims legitimacy as a map of reality. Reality is flux, while power, always trying to preserve itself, insists on the permanence of forms; so form falls ever more at variance with the changing reality it claims faithfully to reflect. Power clings to form even after form's claim to truth has become manifest travesty. The emperor has no clothes.

We are not suited to be free. We are suited still, as when we were children, to live under the protection of, and within the limits set by, loving parents. As adults we strive to continue this arrangement, with kings and gods slipping into the place of parents.

Always we are of two minds about power. Because we are insecure, we need someone above us, more powerful than we, to whom we can turn for protection and guidance. So great is this need that it shapes our perception: we see our wise men as wiser than they are, our kings as more kingly, our priests as more holy. Being themselves but human, and having the same needs as we, they, too, are driven to look upward, to find someone or something more powerful than they. So we have gods. We kneel, we pray to an Almighty.

At the same time we distrust all power, know that it may not protect but exploit, may use us for its own ends. So we are poised for rebellion. When the wind veers, we will turn upon our leaders, tear them apart. The bodies of Mussolini and his mistress, strung up by the heels, swing from the lamppost in Milan.

Neurosis is inhibition and anxiety. And what is normality? The freedom to love and to work. So we say. But is there not something disingenuous about this jaunty loftiness? What are we hiding? Normality is the free pursuit of power—curbed, in deference to prevailing morality, only enough to maintain appearances and to keep us out of trouble.

The child grabs for power in whatever ways spontaneously suggest themselves to him, and in so doing encounters disapproval, punishment, loss of love—so bringing it about that the mere inclination toward forbidden behaviors causes fear, counsels caution. Eventually the parental prohibitions, installed as conscience, operate from within, honored as duty, enforced by guilt, elevated as right and as good.

Morality is fear that has been transformed into conscience. The morality that is observed, as distinct from the morality that is but professed, measures the freedom that individuals have surrendered to the collective in return for security.

The will to power impels the rush of life; morality and fear constitute the barrier; the outcome in behavior is a compromise.

If the barrier is massive, the inhibition or deflection of drive may be so great that no trace of power will stain the goal in view. But however masked or attenuated or denied, hunger for power is the source—for the selfless, the anchorite, the martyr, and the saint, no less than for the man on horseback.

We say we want freedom and justice, and surely we do; but when the tyrant is overthrown and the palace ransacked, the triumphant leaders of the revolution proceed to consolidate that power which was, all along, the unavowed aim ulterior to freedom and justice.

We sicken of power, would give it up, forsake it. We push it away, avert our faces. We try to locate the moving principle of life in love or spirit or service or sacrifice. But power is inalienable. Renounced, it turns out to have been not renounced but cloaked. One simply reaches a point in the pursuit of power at which fear or scruple calls a halt. And there, at that point, inhibited from further pursuit, holding fast to what one has, one arrives at an uneasy equilibrium, alert to depredations equally from those who have more and from those who have less.

Each of us, all of us, every moment of our lives, eating or trying not to be eaten, pursuing or fleeing, struggling to achieve power or dodging its hammer blows—or huddled uneasily at some halfway position.

The way to live should issue, not only from our nature, but also from the nature of the world in which we live, the world that is shaped by the will to power of groups.

A thought experiment.

I am alone in the world. I have always been alone. Nothing and no one to protect me. Just my wits and my strength and such weapons as I find or contrive. In the driving wind the freezing rain is like arrows.

I find a cave—a cave, I discover, that has been found

already by a bear. I will drive him out if I can. I do not think: This is not fair, it belongs to him. I do not wonder: Who has the greater need, he or I? I drive him out.

I am hungry; a fawn comes within range of my stone. I do not ponder contending rights, do not weigh the fawn's life against my own; I kill.

I am warm; I am full, the day is over, I lie down to sleep. I keep my club close to hand.

One day I encounter another man. I cannot read his gestures or understand his strange sounds. I give him a wide berth, go my own way. He follows. I make threatening gestures, he retreats. At night I do not sleep well. How close is he? What does he intend? The next day, at my bidding, he comes closer. I kill him.

For the solitary savage, should ever such a creature have existed, there is no guilt, no right and no wrong.

Years pass. Millennia. Now I live in a community. There are thirty or forty of us. We hunt together, sit around the fire together, are frightened as one by the evil spirits of the forest. Within this group I do not kill, do not steal, do not deceive. I am no longer free, I live within limits, I have become moral.

Another group moves into our territory. They are fishing in our streams, killing our game. One of our men is found with an arrow in his back. We lament, we wail, we rage. Our chief calls a council. We are endangered, he tells us; our way of life is threatened; we must avenge our loss. We beat our drums to drive away our fear, paint horizontal stripes of red and white on our bodies. At midnight we set forth. In silence and stealth we approach the sleeping camp. We drink strong beer. Two boys with torches set fire to the straw huts. As the occupants rush out, silhouetted by the flames, we let loose our arrows, our spears. When our enemies are in blind panic, we fall upon them, club them to death. Some of the women we rape; we throw the babies into the fire; we kill everybody, burn everything. On the march home we are content, relaxed, fulfilled. We sing, we laugh, we are triumphant.

The members of the group have become moral, they live within limits, while for the group itself there is no good and no evil.

Morality is conservative, aims to preserve what is valuable in life. Meaning, therefore, must be antecedent to morality. For meaning establishes value. If life is without meaning, there is nothing worth preserving: All is equal, anything goes.

What binds us together in a community is shared beliefs. Vital yet unnoticed, like the air we breathe, they constitute the meaning of life, tell us how to interpret our experience, determine *what* we experience. With them we grasp the world, make sense of what happens to us, find our place, arrange our lives into known patterns. We feel at home; we know how to live. They constitute our scheme of things.

But something is left over. Something of bereavement or pain or mystery is unaccounted for, experience of which we cannot make sense, with which we cannot come to terms. This is the *margin of terror*. If we are loyal to the received wisdom, we look away, pretend it does not exist, is of no importance, a deviation, a neurosis perhaps; experience is falsified, but the scheme of things is not impugned. The received wisdom spreads its sheltering umbrellas.

If one is loyal to deviant experience, to the pain and the mystery, one is apostate to the common faith and hence estranged from those who live by it, which is pretty much everybody. One finds oneself alone in a desert where one's specialness is scant comfort.

Nothing stays. The world would fling us away, spins like a carousel. Do you know? Do you feel it, this losing of grip? The received interpretations no longer work, don't fit, don't take hold. We cannot grasp the world.

Some people don't hear the screaming; the old fictions still work. Some hear it keenly: The chalk has worn down, the fingernail drags across an endless blackboard, the sky is empty.

In times of peace most people find it possible to believe, at least nominally, in the received wisdom. In times of great social upheaval—the Napoleonic Wars, the Russian Revolution—the received wisdom is shattered for everyone. The world is lost—because it was those shared beliefs, now overturned and discredited, that constituted the world.

Our holiest fictions designate what is right and what is wrong, constitute a scheme of things that redeems the way things are. The way things are is the will to power of groups. The scheme of things conceals the ways of power behind a lofty and glittering facade. The whole system hangs on the efficacy of images and words, the keeping of promises, the observance of convention.

The reign of order, Valéry writes, which is that of symbols and signs, always results in fairly general disarmament, "beginning with visible arms and gradually spreading to the will. Swords get thinner and vanish, characters get rounder. The age when fact was dominant fades imperceptibly away. Under the names *foresight* and *tradition,* the future and the past, which are imaginary perspectives, dominate and restrain the present."

We must note, however, as Valéry does not, that the general disarmament is only *within* the system of order. The brutality and barbarism of the individual have but passed to the collective. The sword of the citizen gets thinner, vanishes; the sword of the state gets longer, sharper.

Parts serve the whole. The organism grows larger and more powerful by virtue of finding better and better ways to exploit its constituents. Slaves may be made to man the oars and drive the galley, but it requires the constant attention of a slave master cracking the whip. But if the slaves can be converted to a faith in the ship and its mission, then no slave master will be needed—he will now be free to help with the cannon—while the ship slices forward ever faster, with more power, more dangerous to its enemies.

There is no alternative to power, no other position—not Christianity nor the Golden Rule nor brotherly love nor nonviolence; not self-sacrifice nor the turning of the other cheek. For all these various abnegations of power by parts of a whole are, unwittingly, in the service of increased power to the whole; and the morality created by such renunciations is used by the aggregate to increase the power with which it then pursues more power.

Good and evil come into existence as defined by power, and are shaped to protect power. They filter down from rulers, magistrates, educators, from bishops, priests, and Sunday school teachers to parents, who shape the conscience of children, imprint the limits, instill the guilt.

Order and safety are maintained; citizens need not bear arms; violence is proscribed, banished beyond borders. And so it comes about that the modern state is thought to be a moral state, even a Christian state, the source and the defender of morality, of civilization, of high culture. But the morality that is here, rightly, ascribed to the state is *internal,* the lawfulness of cells within an organism. In its conduct with other states, and with those barbarians beyond its borders, the state is a killer. And utterly self-righteous in its exterminations. The state claiming morality is like a murderer claiming innocence by pointing out that his hands and feet moved lawfully during the performance of the crime.

The state does not intend *itself* to become moral; it requires morality of its subjects as the necessary basis of its own amoral power, of its continued ability to conduct international brigandage abroad and the torture of political prisoners at home.

The unselfishness of individuals empowers the selfishness of states. The selflessness of patriots becomes the arrogance of nations. Morality constricts and diminishes the life of the individual as it strengthens and enlarges the life of the collective.

The cohesiveness of the group, achieved by the morality and lawfulness of its constituents, enables the group to become larger and stronger. The morality of the individual thus has survival value for the amoral collective and, insofar as the safety of the individual depends upon the power of the collective, also for the individual.

But the group can never, as a group, govern itself, cannot organize and exploit its potential power. For this, leaders are required, leaders with a vision of how the group may become even stronger. And such leaders can appear only if certain individuals within the morally organized collective are themselves immoral, break the rules in pursuit of personal power. So the greatest chance of survival falls, paradoxically, to that collective which has achieved solidarity by morality and, at the same time, contains within itself a leaven of opportunists who will exploit that morality for personal power.

He who wants power must be prepared to live flexibly between respecting rules and violating rules. Never must he break rules so flagrantly as to be flung out of the hierarchy; for the outcast will remain powerless. Since power can be gained only *within* the hierarchy, it is imperative that he remain in good standing with that part of the structure above him. Yet never must he observe the rules so respectfully as to miss the chance to seize unmerited

advancement, to climb *over*, and perhaps dislodge, someone above him on the ladder.

Commitment to a social cause conveys license to an individual to reach for power with a ruthlessness forbidden to
purely personal interest. And the greater one's individual
sacrifice in the service of that cause, the greater the license.

Hitler wept in shame and humiliation as Germany
surrendered to the Allies in 1918. Suddenly he was
enveloped in darkness, was blind. "Only now did I realize," he wrote later, "how all personal suffering vanished
in comparison with the misfortune of the Fatherland."
He made a solemn vow: Should he regain his sight, he
would consecrate his life to the resurrection of Germany.
Voices summoned him. And then the miracle: He could
see again. For what he proceeded thereafter to do he
claimed the sanction of God.

From horde to clan to city to state, the progression is the
function of a constant will to power acting on an accel-
erating progression of technological means. The spread of
Christianity does not war with this process, but serves it;
for Christianity, by way of the morality it fosters, supports
the solidarity of the masses and thereby the increased
power of the state.

State power contends with individual power. The hunger for power by the collective, with the aim of ruthless conquest, leads it to demand of the individual a morality of self-sacrifice, a willingness to die for the state, whereas the hunger for power in an individual leads him to ignore, insofar as he can do so safely, the morality required of him by the collective.

The state exercises enormous power; the individual, even the very powerful individual, relatively little. It comes about, therefore, that those individuals who are gifted and able, and who in the pursuit of power are not much burdened by loyalty to shared beliefs, who indeed are skilled at professing and representing these beliefs while at the same time violating them in pursuit of personal aggrandizement . . . those people strive for and achieve leadership and come thereby to be in the position of controlling and directing the enormous power of the state.

And just as the individual in his quest of personal power is likely not to announce his aim as such, perhaps not even to himself, but rather to advance it euphemistically ("I want to work with people"; "I am interested in research"; "I seek a career in public service"), so those who determine the actions of the state likewise disguise the nature of those acts. They speak of securing national safety, of serving national interest, of supporting democracy in third world countries, of ensuring civil rights, of preserving our democratic heritage; but under cover of these revered principles and these professed purposes the state acts to enlarge its power.

What prevents the achievement in reality of peaceful social arrangements throughout the world is not chance, not fate, not stupidity, not individual error or wrong-doing, but the unlimited will to power of sovereign states. What makes for the inherent absurdity of great collective events, such as wars and revolutions, is that the will to power of nations, and the actions to which it leads them, and the consequences of these actions, bear no relation to any reasonable goal of human conscience. So the individual of goodwill, with his ideals of peace, freedom, justice, equality—or even, more modestly, of simple common sense—is confronted with something with which he cannot come to terms, an unfathomable and unyielding absurdity.

Power is protean. When, during the Cuban Missile Crisis, the United States and the Soviet Union squared off against each other, the power of each was a function of bombs, ships, missiles, planes, tanks, armored divisions. These were the factors that each had to reckon with as it braced itself for struggle. But within each nation the enormous power, respectively, of Kennedy and of

Khrushchev was charismatic, depending upon the ability of each to inspire belief that he individually did possess those magical powers which the peoples of those countries had as children experienced in their fathers and now unconsciously imputed to their leaders.

In February 1942 Hitler stood at the podium in the Sportpalast and addressed ten thousand young newly appointed lieutenants in the Wehrmacht and the Waffen SS. He told them truthfully of the disastrous reverses in Russia: two hundred thousand German soldiers had already been killed, seven hundred thousand wounded, fifty thousand were missing, one hundred thousand disabled with frostbite. He told them it was their great and holy mission to save Germany and Western civilization from the Communist hordes.

The young officers were sitting in that vast hall looking up at the author of the war in which millions of their countrymen had already perished, and this man was now sending them east, where most of them would fall in mud and blood. Yet his speech moved them deeply, aroused a profound patriotic passion. Many began to weep. He evoked and shaped in them a mood of fervent devotion and self-sacrifice. As they listened, more and more they *wanted* to go. It would be a great honor to die for such a leader. He who had created the danger that now so gravely threatened them was able to present himself convincingly as the father who would always protect them, even as he dispatched them to their deaths.

The new lieutenants had been ordered not to applaud, but when Hitler started down the aisle, they could not restrain themselves. They cheered wildly, many of them leaping onto their chairs the better to see him.

Most significant power is composite, being both instrumental and charismatic. Instrumental power is that which accrues in consequence of competence at the work of the world—the growing of wheat, the building of houses, the designing of an airplane, the composing of a sonnet. The smaller the extent of power, the more likely it is to be instrumental. The greater the power, the more likely it is to be charismatic. A Hitler, a Churchill, a Napoleon is likely to hold power primarily by virtue of his ability to embody protection from our deepest fears and gratification of our primitive and grandiose fantasies, and perhaps not at all by virtue of competence at directing the affairs of a nation. Indeed, some such leaders, far from being competent to govern, lead the nations for which they are responsible straight to destruction.

Once nature was the danger and the challenge. The cave drawings of Stone Age man bear witness to his preoccupying concern with animals as a source of food and as a source of danger. The ability to elude these animals, to capture or to kill them, was the locus of power. Now anyone can shoot a rifle, no animal poses a threat, the ability to fell a charging elephant wins us no fame, perhaps even contempt, and we know that we may, if careless, destroy animals utterly. Most significant power now is power over people. The ability to win the respect, the belief, the support, the allegiance, the following, the obedience, of people—this is power.

Morality, law, and custom comprise the rules by which the group expects us, as individuals, to live. These rules allow for a modest accumulation of power by way of instrumental competence. If we respect the rules, we cannot hope for more. We shall be conformists, the salt of the earth but never its giants.

A more venturesome order of normality calls for one to be as free in pursuit of power as a prudent, though often but nominal, regard for rules will permit. With less than that prudent regard, one is likely to land in disfavor or in jail—though sometimes, with a little luck, an adventurous thug may become a ruler. With more than a prudent regard one is handicapped in the race.

Neurotics are those who are crippled in the pursuit of power by internal constraints, impediments built into character by childhood experience. All of us start out weak in the hands of the strong, and a parent inclined to

exploit that discrepancy can teach a child that any trans-
gression of rules will yield pain and humiliation. Such an
early education can bring it about that in later life, long
after the tyrant is dead, any tentative reaching for power
will be aborted by anxiety.

The awareness of vulnerability prompts one to look
about carefully, to take the measure of things. It leads to
knowledge, is essential to good judgment. Without it
one's vision of one's self and the world is determined, not
by the way things are but by one's will, one's desire. When
power is absolute, distortion is extreme; the real world is
replaced by fantasy.

In April 1942 Hitler, already possessed of greater
power than any despot of the past, appeared before
the Reichstag to ask for ultimate power: Every German
was henceforth to follow his personal order or suffer
death. The Reichstag deputies enthusiastically and unan-
imously approved the measure. He was now, legally,
above any law.

So empowered, and thereby more and more out of
touch with the reality he was imperiously undertaking to
shape and to control, and with no compunction to heed
the advice of his generals, who *were* in touch, he proceeded to make those disastrous mistakes which led to
the destruction of the Sixth Army at Stalingrad and the
loss of the war in the East.

Nothing within the state impedes the pursuit of power by the state. Empires expand. Any one of them, were it able, would encompass the world. They go as far as they can, stop only where the lines of communication and supply are stretched too thin, where the conduits of power can no longer deliver effective force.

In the individual, however, morality is a brake and may at any point set a limit. A truly Christian position calls for the abnegation of power, requires one to give all he has to the poor, to be meek, to love his enemy, to turn the other cheek. A measure of the instinctual force of the drive for power is given by the rarity with which such an ethic has in fact been practiced.

The other internal obstacle is fear. One can go quite far in the acquisition of instrumental power without struggling with another human being and hence without encountering fear, power growing as a function of one's skill in becoming a good pianist, carpenter, bookkeeper, or surgeon. But a point is reached eventually beyond which any further gain can be achieved only in struggle with another person, in defeating or besting or outmaneuvering someone. In such contest one is vulnerable, there is no sure win. One may show one's self a fool, may be humiliated. Fear may become so intense that one's life comes to be structured around it. Whoever arranges for himself an isolated life (a writer, an artist, a forest-fire watcher, a drawbridge keeper) or a vocation with built-in advantages over the people with whom one deals (a psychoanalyst, an anesthesiologist) is likely to be one who feels keenly the danger of pursuing power through inter-personal struggle.

The hurdy-gurdy plays, and around and around they go, the charioteer, the legionnaire, the cuirassier, up and down, sailing around, the president, the foreign minister, the chiefs of staff, varnished faces frozen in arrogance and disdain, the bombardier, the cavalryman, the machine gunner, around and around, as the band plays on.

When the oppressed take up arms and rebel, they do so in the name of principles that assert basic human rights and so constitute an insurgent morality which justifies the overthrow of the existing order. The existing order has a morality of its own, an establishment morality, which holds that the security and welfare of each individual are contingent on the state, that the state therefore is owed allegiance, that its laws must be obeyed, its leaders respected. It labels the leaders of the rebellion as traitors, criminals, fanatics, and will crush them if it can. As rebels confront government troops, so insurgent morality confronts establishment morality. If government troops prevail, the insurgent morality is discredited, disappears. If the rebels are victorious, the establishment morality is discredited, succeeded by the insurgent morality.

In the latter event the insurgent morality comes to be allied with power, becomes the new establishment morality, ancillary to the safeguarding and expansion of power. In this new role it sanctifies power, reassures the now newly oppressed that their oppression is in the nature of things, perhaps ordained by divine will, that no protest is indicated but rather patience and cooperation, that all must make sacrifices, that the leaders act for the welfare of all, that laws must be obeyed.

Thus a morality which began as protest against power becomes the servant of power. The insurgent morality in its insurgency declares that power is corrupt and tends to corrupt everyone and everything allied to it; and when the revolution succeeds, it proves the truth of its indictment by corrupting first those exalted principles under whose banners it rode to power, along with the warriors who bore them.

The merry-go-round spins, and around and around they go, the missileman, the submariner, the minister of propaganda, up and down, around and around, while the band plays on.

Those persons who arrive at the intermediate ranges of power have clean hands, white lace cuffs. They are doctors, jurists, writers, scientists, artists, editors, professors, poets. They delegate to others the bloodier, the more immediately cruel and exploitative aspects of power. Thereby they create a space around themselves in which can flourish the gentler sentiments: love, empathy, pity, even self-sacrifice. These gentler sentiments then gradually generate a morality which condemns the unfettered will to power.

People of this sequestered moral group increasingly criticize those more distant agencies which execute the will of the state, thereby becoming estranged from the source of their own security and their affluence. Power becomes alien to them. They see it as brutal, abhorrent. They say the state is immoral—which it is. Increasingly they use their influence to restrict the state in its exercise of power over its constituents and over other states.

Thus an enclave of the privileged, who have distanced themselves from the bloody hands to which they owe their privileged state, articulates a morality that would manacle those hands.

A powerful society can afford, may even support and defend, such an enclave of the morally fastidious. But if the message of this minority should persuade the whole, the whole would find itself in peril. For force, as John Keegan has remarked, provides the ultimate constraint whereby all settled societies protect themselves against the enemies of order within and without. Those persons with the knowledge and will to use force stand close to the center of any society's power structure; power holders who lack such will or knowledge will find themselves driven from that center. Mercenaries will fight alongside citizen soldiers; but if there *are* no citizen soldiers, if all citizens maintain clean hands and all dirty work is delegated to mercenaries, then not for long will mercenaries be content to fight for wages. Wielding the force, they will proceed to take the power. Force, like a heat-seeking missile, finds out those who lack the will to use it.

V

Sovereignty

Order derives from authority. When authority is lost we are free, everything is permitted, nothing is worthwhile, and we live in chaos. When the police disappear, looting sweeps through the streets.

We can stand evil and cruelty; what we cannot stand is lack of order. If the reigning scheme of things is intact, that is, *believed* in, and thereby endowed with authority, then we can tolerate murder and mayhem to uphold it. But if the scheme of things falls, leaving us in unlimited freedom, we churn about in chaos until rescued by some other creed that claims our allegiance, takes our freedom, and restores order.

Evil springs up here, there, everywhere, all the time, flows, equally, from the breaking of rules and from the too-careful observance of old rules in a changed society.

The evil wrought by those who intend evil is negligible. The greater evil is wrought by those who intend good, and are convinced they know how to bring it about; and the greater their power to bring it about, the greater the evil they achieve while trying to do it. Not content modestly to oppose evil, they in their arrogance undertake to eliminate it completely, thereby creating greater evil. The war to end all wars prepares the way for bigger wars, for destructions more vast.

An animal lives its life according to its nature and its circumstances, and therefore is never in the position of having to conclude that it has wasted its life. But a human being, out of fear of breaking the rules, may waste his life, may observe himself being afraid to live it.

We live within limits. We know that life must be lived, and experience must be confined, within these limits.

Fear God is the command sounding throughout the Old Testament. Fear God and respect God and bow down before God—these injunctions mean: Keep away from those boundaries. Murder is the privilege of God, not of man. The burning of cities, the turning of a woman into a pillar of salt, the destruction of the world by flood—all this is at the discretion, or the whim, of God, but not of man.

We should note, however, that it is only human beings as individuals who are required to observe these limits. Human collectives have always ignored them. Rape and murder and the burning of cities, proclaimed as activities reserved to God, are routinely undertaken by sovereign human collectives.

Fear, as well as morality, opposes the individual will to power, and often it is unclear whether it is morality setting the limit, or fear masquerading as morality.

Because we are afraid, we live in groups. Alone one is weak; in the crowd one will become strong. If the crowd grows rapidly and achieves great density, a moment of discharge will arrive, leveling hierarchies of power, making all equal; there will be no one above giving orders, making us feel weak and afraid, because everything above will be destroyed; we will surge through the streets, smashing windows and doors, overturning police cars, burning palaces.

When men live each on his own, should ever this have been the case, morality does not exist. Such men have freedom without limit, but the enjoyment of that freedom is slight; for each must be on guard against all others, and each must scrounge alone for food and shelter.

It appears advantageous for all, therefore, if each surrenders a bit of freedom in exchange for group solidarity. So each gives up his right to murder, to steal, to deceive. Now all are less free but more safe. Without fear they live together, secure against predators, hunt more successfully in a group, build better shelters.

The group comes into being by collecting the surrendered rights of its constituent individuals. The group itself surrenders nothing, is subject to no rule, is free to use its aggregate force for such acts of murder, of stealing, of deceiving, as it may see fit. And it does often so see fit. The members of the group have become moral; the group is now the predator. The individual restraints consequent to surrendered individual freedoms constitute the stuff of morality.

The aggregate power of the surrendered rights is exercised not by all acting in concert but by rulers. We hope that the freedoms we have surrendered will be exercised by our rulers for the benefit of all. Such is rarely the case.

The relationship of the individual to the state is not that of cell to multicellular organism. For the cell surrenders *all* autonomy to the organism, whereas the individual person withholds some initiative from the state. The state, in its will to power, would have it that individuals become like cells; and occasionally, when the state is exceedingly powerful, it may bring this about. The autonomy we retain as individuals constitutes a limit to the degree to which the state may command our compliance.

The extent to which the individual is committed to the shared beliefs of his community measures the extent to which he has been willing to give up individual power in the interests of community. When shared beliefs are firm, the collective wields great power, its constituents correspondingly less. When shared beliefs are destroyed, the collective loses power.

At the top of the hierarchy of social organization is the realm of sovereignty, where there is no effective constraint. Here the hypocrisy is extreme; for the security of the collective is dependent upon the confidence of its constituents that the government is itself bound by those principles which protect its constituents, as well as its neighbors, from the abuse of its power. So the spokesmen for the sovereign amoral nation are constantly proclaiming the nation's morality, its commitment to justice, freedom, and peace, whereas in fact they are leading the nation in the pursuit of more power by whatever means promise success. Insofar as this pursuit is curbed at all, it is curbed by fear of retaliation by other sovereign states and fear of insurrection at home.

The proclaiming of morality by the state is so loud and so constant, becomes such a litany, that the leaders of a nation may hypnotize themselves, may come to believe their own public relations act. Concurrent with careful plotting for the annexation of the Philippine Islands, the American government advanced the fiction that the unpredictable fortunes of war were making America the unwilling and reluctant recipient and custodian of the islands. And when, later, the conquest achieved, a group of clergymen called upon President McKinley, he explained just how he had arrived at his decision: "I walked the floor of the White House night after night until midnight; and I am not ashamed to tell you gentlemen that I went on my knees and prayed to Almighty God for light and guidance more than one night. And one night it came to me this way—that there was nothing left for us to do but to take them all, and to educate the Filipinos, and uplift and civilize and Christianize them. And by God's grace do the very best we could by them, as our fellowmen for whom

Christ also died. And then I went to bed and went to sleep and slept soundly."

Morality is not a vision of ends, however desirable, but a system of restraints in the pursuit of any end. States speak the language of morality without the intention of being limited by it. They behave as they see fit, and the way they see fit is then declared to be moral. If they embark on conquest, it is in "self-defense." If they invade and take over a neighboring state, it is at the "invitation" of that state to maintain order, liberty, justice, etc. Since there is no tribunal with the authority to disallow such claims, the state has the last word. And its last word is always a pious assertion of morality.

When we condemn, as we often do, the action of a sovereign entity as wrong—the torture of political prisoners, for example—we do so on the basis of an individual morality that obtains *within* the collective. We extend those limits, rules, and restraints, and demand that the state itself observe them.

And how does the challenged state respond? It says: "Like all civilized nations, we absolutely condemn the torture of political prisoners. Be assured it does not happen here." When presented with names, dates, photographs: "These regrettable incidents were the unauthorized actions of certain guards, who will be apprehended and punished."When it is demonstrated that the practice continues: "We do it only when absolutely necessary for national security." When pressed further: "Other nations do it, too, including your own." And finally: "Your visa is canceled. Go home."

So what then does it mean when we condemn a state for evil acts? It means that we believe there *should* be limits, rules, to which the state is subject, however lofty the ends in view which might call for their suspension, and that if it does not conform to these limits, it should be forcibly restrained and punished. Which is to say, there *should* be a morality of sovereign states. And so perhaps there should. But there *is* not. And should ever it come about, the states it restrained would no longer be sovereign.

A double standard is unavoidably at work in the life of a strong and flourishing state: Its citizens observe limits in their conduct with each other, whereas for the state nothing is forbidden. If individuals in the pursuit of their private aims were to consider themselves as free of limits as Machiavelli's Prince in his conduct of the state, nothing being absolutely forbidden, then the actions of these individuals would immediately reduce society to chaos. The state would have become a mob; the Prince would have nothing to rule.

People have always believed—have seemed driven and determined, in the face of overwhelming countervailing evidence, to believe—that moral society as well as moral individual life is possible; that however rare or partial its actual achievement, it is in principle possible for individuals to live morally with the advantages of security, order, and opportunity provided by a powerful state, and for that state itself to behave morally with its constituents and with its neighbors. It was the accomplishment of Machiavelli, in a kind of Godel's proof of political economy, to show that such is not the case, that the good and moral life within an orderly society is contingent on the amorality of the state that makes it possible.

When individuals come together to form a social entity, there must be a period during which the association is revocable; the individuals may find themselves subject to more constraint than they are willing to accept, and may opt out. This revocable period is the hinge of life or death for the social organism; for if the individuals disperse, the larger entity disappears. This larger entity, driven by its own will to power, will therefore do everything it can to end this period of revocability as quickly as possible; for so soon as the association achieves such specialization as to make it impossible for the parts to opt out and survive, at just that point the association becomes irrevocable, and the organism no longer in danger of perishing by virtue of the willed dispersion of its components.

Aggregates, therefore, always act to increase the dependence of member components. The aggregate wants to bring it about that when the aggregate itself is endangered, its component parts will have no choice but to remain loyal. My country right or wrong.

When the mountain men came down out of the Rockies in the nineteenth century and took up life in the village, there was a period in which, if community constraints proved too onerous, they could pack back into the mountains and resume their isolated and independent existences. The present-day citizen of Denver or Butte or Taos has lost this option, is no longer capable of wilderness survival, and is held, moreover, by ties to the union or the grange, to the American Legion or the Rotary Club, and by Social Security, whence will come his pension.

The aggregate is not satisfied, however, to have its component parts stick together only because they could not survive on their own. Such allegiance is halfhearted. ("We have a terrible president, the country is on a disastrous course, but I guess we have to rally behind him. We have no choice.") The aggregate wants to generate patriotic fervor, to bring it about that individuals lose sight of their separate lives, lose awareness of their ubiquitous conflict with the state, that their identification with the state expunge the purview of individual life with its joys and sorrows, its hopes, its ideals, and particularly its ability to criticize the state in terms of reason, of common sense, and of the discrepancy between the announced aims of the state and the actions the state is undertaking. The unison of *Sieg Heil* by the packed and disciplined masses at Nuremburg, that is what the state wants; or the faith of Nikolai Rostov, who in holy warlike exaltation charges forward alone, an embodiment of the Russian spirit, against the massed French forces at Austerlitz. Think not of what your country can do for you, said President Kennedy, but of what you can do for your country.

There is, therefore, a constant struggle between the individual and the state. For the state to gain power, individuals must lose power. The state would like to eat up *all* individual power, all independence, discretion, freedom, autonomy. The individual opposes this demand, insists that the state not take any more. In times of danger to the state, however, individuals can be persuaded to relinquish additional bits of freedom, since the security of the individual rests ultimately with the security of the state. In a crisis we vote war credits and military conscription. And the state, knowing this, is always tempted to create crises that will justify arrogating to itself additional increments of the independence of its components.

In this continuing struggle, the last century has witnessed a decisive shift in favor of the state. The Fascist and Communist movements since 1917 managed to appropriate vastly more power than citizens had ever in the past been willing to give up. The values of art, of individual conscience, of personal preference and belief, all presumably secure within the private realm, have in our times been confiscated by the state.

Nor is this a vicissitude; it is a tendency. A tendency made almost invincible by modern technology, which, by virtue of its ever-increasing size, cost, complexity, and power, is, in this conflict, intrinsically on the side of the state. The nature of modern commerce and communication automatically empower the state at the expense of the individual.

Television exerts a steady pressure on the private person to live in the public world, in the ambience of the aggregate, with the values and the assumptions of the aggregate, rather than in the private sphere. Whatever is being shown on the screen, whether debates or advertising or talk shows, the viewer is always being instructed on how to live in the public world, while the private world is being subtly and insidiously impugned, is being made to disappear.

We in America like to think that our government is accountable. We are relieved when the president, though gaining power at an alarming rate, is reined in by Congress or the courts. But as we take comfort in the prudence of our constitutional checks and balances, we fail to note that nothing limits the action of the state as a whole. If the president and Congress concur in an action, then, though it be a monstrous crime, we will do it. At no time has this nation been willing to subject itself to the authority of a world court. We are willing to give an accounting of our actions to the United Nations, but if that body brands our account as lies—as at times it is— we will ignore the stricture and go our own way.

Morality constrains individuals to serve the interests of power for the collective, in the way cells serve the interests of power for the individual. The man may be a killer, but he expects the parts of his body to be law-abiding. If one of his cells decides to follow its own lights, the man will correctly see this as a danger to the whole, will call it a "wild" cell, a cancer, and will destroy it if he can.

It has always been in the interest of power to conceal that morality is its handmaiden; we are trained by power to be blind to this subservience. The official version is as follows: *Morality is independent of power. It may be overcome by power but never invalidated by power. The paradigm of morality is a man with a principle saying no to a man with a gun. It is always possible to say no to evil. That refusal is authorized by conscience, the voice of God within us. We know that some things must not be done. Every man is responsible, is accountable to his fellow man and to God.* We are justified, by these lights, in hanging men who do not say no. The Nazi warlords should have said no to Hitler. The sovereign state of Israel solemnly examined the evidence and decided that Eichmann should have said no.

The official version is a lie. The Nuremberg trials were public relations. The trials of Adolf Eichmann and of Lieutenant Calley were public relations. They were meant to demonstrate to the world that *our* states, the Western allies and Israel, are moral as sovereign entities. It is a lie: To be moral is to be subject to restraint; to be sovereign is to do as one sees fit. Israel is sovereign, does as it sees fit, and it does *not* want its high-level administrators to say no; it expects them, Eichmann-like, to implement policy. The United States does *not* want its ministers and generals to say no; once the course of action has been set, it expects them to follow through. We expect our lieutenants to do what their captains tell them to do. And we have any number of trained and loyal officers ready to perform as ordered when ordered to launch the missiles that will kill millions.

WAYS OF

THE HEART

VI

Desire

Cape Cod, August, bright sun, warm sand, children, beach blankets, sling chairs, bikinis, sunscreen, nymphets, novels.

I find a table at the edge of the terrace, sit beneath an orange umbrella. Next to me is an Italian family: a young man, slender, tanned, athletic, handsome in the manner of Rudolf Valentino, his wife and baby, and a corpulent older woman with dyed red hair, sedately eating ice cream—the wife's mother, I think, an image perhaps of what is in store for her. A small black and white dog is gnawing at a tennis ball.

The young woman is seated under a red umbrella at the table beside me. "How old is the baby?" I ask.

For a moment she is blank, then realizes that I am speaking to her in English and, to her delight, that she understands. A dazzling smile. "Eight months," she says.

I am astonished, exclaim about the baby, how beautiful. She holds my eyes, knows I speak rather of her. I study her lithe and girlish figure, the small waist, the firm belly. She wears a low-cut black halter, thin black shoulder straps, silken smooth nut-brown skin.

Now she lies on her back in the grass, holds the baby up in the air before her. Brief brown shorts, long slender legs. She rocks the baby side to side in her hands, coos at him, squints against the sun. The strap slips off her left shoulder, the almost exposed breast lies before me. The umbrella bathes her flesh in a dark flush. I watch the play of expressions across her face, take in her lips, her nose, the dark liquid eyes, the dark hair. She brings the baby down to her face, then rapidly up in the air again, rocks him side to side, down to her face again, plays with his face with her own face, rubbing noses, mouths, ears, foreheads. She glances at me, smiles. I think she knows she is torturing me, making me want to do with her what she is doing with the baby.

I turn away from her. The green meadow slopes down to a rushing stream. I look up at the blue sky, white clouds drifting peacefully. All is calm around me, blissful, pastoral. Why am I caught up in such agitation? Why do I pursue such a mad fantasy? What am I after?

Before me is a line from Max Frisch: " . . . the world withdrawn into its future without me, and so this narrowing down to the I which knows itself excluded from the common experience of the future. All that remains is the mad desire for present identity through a woman."

I feel weightless. Would I, if adored, acquire substance? Yes. I do seek this—or something like this—through a woman. These fantasies are anti-mortality dreams.

It's my interiority I'm trying to save, my spirit, my soul. Consciousness is going to end. That's what I protest, the waste. And not just mine but mine multiplied into eternity. Whenever anyone dies, anyone, just such a vast, unique, irreplaceable weight of knowing and of spirit plunges into nothingness. The universe is a charnel house, a cataract of soul pours unendingly over the brink. We all swim upstream against the overpowering current, ever more doomed and desperate, trying at the last moment to throw something ashore, some little thing that will remain, bear witness that we were here.

I marvel at this girl. Mid-twenties, perhaps, so fruitful, and yet—eight months after childbirth—pristine, slim-waisted, virginal. Could be her wedding day. I am full of admiration. And dizzy. My mouth is suddenly dry. She takes my breath away, is beginning to drive me mad. She glances at me. The pain begins.

I veer away—to her mother: corpulent, mid-forties, a short generation removed, yet already far, far from her daughter. Nothing left of that dangerousness, that mystery. Flaccid, slowly licking her ice cream, all of sexuality behind her, her only remaining adventure being vanity, and the changing color of hair.

It doesn't work, I'm already caught. I try once more to dodge it, turn my attention to the young man. Early twenties, lithe, muscular, dark curly hair. About six feet, a skier perhaps, or a dancer. Perfectly sculptured features, dark skin—more likely a model!—anyway an Adonis, and knows it, his manner and expression serene, perhaps indolent. Nothing in him of my incompleteness, my yearning, my passion; he is content to be the object of desire. Were I of a different disposition I might swoon over him. For a moment I try, put myself in the mood of Aschenbach in *Death in Venice*. It doesn't work. My take on this boyish beauty is detached, uncaring; it means nothing to me.

Then I give up. No way to avoid it or abort it. I'm already caught, am being swept away, know with a kind of mournful inevitability what I'm in for.

I turn back to her. Again she glances at me. I see in her eyes recognition of what I feel—which but confirms her expectation, she knew without looking. Good. And what does *she* feel? Is she triumphant? What do I *want* her to feel? I want her acknowledgment of a special connection between us, a sign, a clue, that she knows something has

begun, that already between us is the germ of something
... what? ... something grand or violent.

A wound, a deep, burning pain, private and somehow
shameful. It can neither be acknowledged nor com-
plained about. It will not go away. A fetid sickness rises
from the cut. This is the cruelty of great beauty, that it
inflicts this wound, that the pain is forever.

The young man gathers up baby, carriage, dog, provi-
sions, and sets off across the meadow with the baby in the
bouncing carriage, followed by the mother-in-law. The
young woman gathers up toys, paper towels, purse, stuffs
everything into a large olive-drab rucksack, swings it over
her right shoulder, glances back at me, "*Arrivederci!*" she
says, and strides off across the meadow after her disap-
pearing family.

I am full of desire. Never straight up, balanced, but always
leaning, I fall in love easily, a small push will do it. And
when it happens I always feel I am possessed by—am in
possession *of*—something unique and precious, something that alone can lift me up out of the flat world of
dailiness into the higher realm for which life must be des-
tined. Then I want desperately for it to last forever. And
when it crumbles, as always it does, I find that I had been
in possession only of something ordinary.

And I never learn. I am, I think, unwilling to learn—

because I cannot help but believe that what leads me on, however disastrously, is nevertheless what is best in me, most worth hanging on to. The alternative, it seems, is a cynicism so trenchant and bitter as to make life impossible.

I understand my ailment but can't seem to change it. Maybe I don't really want to recover. Maybe that is the secret and sinister nature of this disease, that one doesn't want to get well.

Sexual coupling is our primary experience. Everything else must give way. It is primary because only thereby can the species extend itself in time. Not that the species, *qua* species, *wants* to live forever. The species doesn't *want* anything. But those individuals disinclined to couple do not reproduce; their genetic lines are lost. While those driven to couple, and smart enough to make it happen frequently, *do* reproduce. Thus a winnowing of genes over vast reaches of time has sculptured us, like wind shaping sandstone, into creatures of desire.

We desire intensely. In a crunch, family, friends, career, honor, even life itself may be swept away.

My plight, my curse, my demon, a savage yearning for something I'm never going to get. Something to redeem me. From what? From vanity, insignificance, transience. From dung and death.

Most of the time I can arrange not to know, but it's always there, lurking, my own beast in the jungle; and sometimes it springs, lays waste my spirit, leaving only shards and rubble of meaning.

When life has meaning, desire is held to its proper place—"proper" being the shape and scope and authority allowed to it by the interlocking structure of values that constitutes the meaning of life. When life is without meaning, desire is a wildfire out of control.

To express desire is to empower the other and disadvantage one's self. Catastrophic if unilateral, exalting when lovers do it together.

But why would they, even together, choose surrender? choose weakness over strength? They seem to *want* to get weaker and weaker, want their legs to give way with love, want to swoon together, fall into each other, totally disappear in each other. They want to die as individuals in the fusion, to be reborn on the other side, a love death followed by magical rebirth. Over and over. And if it is never actually achieved, desire ensures that we keep on trying.

But no matter the pain, one must never seek to be without desire. To desire nothing is to be dead. The glory of life—and there is no other—lies in the desiring of something so much that one will do one's utmost to achieve it, spending the self, going all the way, holding nothing back.

When, in the evolution of human life, consciousness so expands that the individual sees himself as separate from the group, unique, possessed of an inner life oriented by fixed memories, living out a personal history that moves toward its own termination, he becomes aware that the sexual drive which impels him so powerfully will not safeguard that uniqueness. Sex is a being used, and used up, and soon discarded, by a life force that cares nothing for the individual. All those monuments and spires, the swooning sonnets, the flaking paint, the crashing chords, are the residue of protest against such waste. Uniqueness and mortality are our condition, impel us to create legacies meant to last forever.

The creative impulse, writes Otto Rank, is antisexual in its yearning for immortality. Whereas Freud had traced the repression of sexuality to social constraint, Rank sees it as driven by an individual dread of death no less inherent in the individual than the sexual impulse itself.

Hers is an offering of self that holds nothing back. Nothing in reserve, she gives it all. No barter, no expectation of return, no maneuvering for advantage, just a sexy, playful, reckless, up-front "I am yours" with the thoughtlessness and vulnerability of a child and a child's improvident generosity. Who could resist such a gift? The fact that it's free both renders it more enchanting and breaks your heart, moves you to an unfamiliar generosity, you want to protect this vulnerable child who can't arrange for her own security.

But what is offered as love, I warn myself, is in fact a camouflaged raid, and if the gift is accepted she will begin to exact in exchange what then is due and payable, the tribute owed the victorious weak by the vanquished strong; and whatever the outcome of those unhappy negotiations, love, it will transpire, will have played no part at all.

A beautiful woman is always in danger of becoming a witch. Because beauty evokes desire, and desire enslaves; and when the slave eventually rebels, the angel who evoked the desire and, as he then sees it, cast the spell, becomes a witch.

"The recurring comforts us," she says, "the singular is tragic, must not be missed. This is singular. Once, only once, never again. I love you. I trust you. I have never, until now, trusted any man. I have become a different woman. The wildness is gone. It was like a storm. All is calm now. All my life I have moved from man to man, denying possession to any. But you have tamed me. No one could have predicted it. I would not have thought it possible. With you I would stay forever."

We sit in silence, facing each other across a small round table inlaid, in abstract geometric design, with pieces of colored leather in dark muted tones. A gardenia floats in a shallow black lacquer dish, the heavy scent rising between us. She looks into my eyes, she stares, unblinking. Her mouth trembles. Her expression changes from longing to adoration to desperate desire.

She does not know me. I do not know her. Desire deceives. We never know the real other out there, know only that other as reshaped by our desire. We take our fantasy, go looking for a suitable place to lodge it, reshaping reality with longing, stumbling through our years, seeking out stand-ins with whom we can act out again the old script, hoping this time for a happy ending, believing all the while that we are into something new.

And in the rain of conflicts to come, I remind myself, my papier-mâché angel will turn into a witch or a drab.

Yet this passion for a falsified other may be the only thing in life really worthwhile. Without it one lives in a world of dailiness, of hearth love, the ordinary love of husband and wife, of parent and child, of friends. Such love may be constant, caring, loyal, may protect against loneliness and despair, provide the only security possible in a world of hazard, all these good things, and it may be, if we were wise, we would settle for it, renouncing that fever in the blood. But it does not transcend, does not lift us up and out, does not take us to the other side. The assumption that it is *always* desirable to see the world as it is may be in error. The undistorted and hence unexalted life may not be worth living.

Desire is endless and unappeasable, is most intense where most forbidden, and is never far from despair.

VII

Fidelity

She is droll, she is funny, she is faithful, it's a good-enough marriage—but I have fallen in love with another woman.

I want to do the right thing.

Morality is living by the rules, but not all rules are compatible. Following one's passionate heart to one's true love is the right thing. Another right thing is fidelity, the shielding of one's mate from jealousy, pain, and despair. Which of these two right things is more right than the other?

Rules are too plentiful, too various. They contradict each other. It's impossible to obey all the rules all the time. Were I to try, I could locate my most outrageous conduct within a set of rules so adroitly chosen as to permit anything.

Nevertheless, even so, I want to be decent about this.

Is that a cop-out? Is "decency" but the refuge of the coward who quails at the hard choice of right and wrong?

I want to be fair to my wife, but fair also to myself. Fairness is equality in the distribution of goods—as when a mother divides a cake in equal portions for her several children. But what if equality is not possible? What if a clear gain for the one is a clear and unavoidable loss to the other?

It is raining. The light is gray. The raindrops streaking the window create an intimate whispering invitation. She is wearing a pale green dress of thin silk. She lowers her eyes, giving me license to look. No bra. I observe the lift of her breasts as she breathes. Under my ardent gaze nipples become visible.

Problems of right and wrong originate right there, with those breasts. We are pretty clear about theft, murder, the beating of children, the torture of animals. It is in the quagmire of sex, in the love and the caring that may or may not spring up around it, the promises we make, the betrayals that follow those promises, the evasions we practice, the lies we tell—here, here is the agony of conscience, the confusion, the hunger for a god to tell us what is right and what is wrong.

But maybe the answer is right before me. Drop all this sophistry. You know what's right. Do it. The answer stares you in the face: obey the rules. The obvious rules, the simple, in-your-face rules. Have we not always known that we can't have everything? Accept the boundaries, live within their limits and restrictions, and the problem of morality will have been solved.

But even the obvious must be examined. Is it sound? If this solution should come to be generally adopted, what consequences would follow?

The man who is serious and conscientious about rule-observing is the perfectly moral man. Upright. Open. Nothing to hide. You know what he stands for, good as his word, you can count on him. He gets to work on time, never calls in sick, is prudent with his assets, exact in contractual obligations, never shades figures on his tax return. No one would know if he took a few discreet liberties here and there, but *he* would know. He *respects* the rules, endows them with authority. No one has to keep an eye on him. A careful and prudent man, temperate, always looking more toward the rules he must be careful to obey than toward the ever-changing world with its shifting dangers and opportunities. He never flirts with a pretty woman, mindful that the slightest step in that direction might lead to adultery.

What sort of world would it be if everybody were like that? Would it be an improvement on the world we have? Might it be heaven?

Certainly it would be different. We would have no more Clintons for sure, nor Kennedys, nor Roosevelts.

It might be that no one I really love would be there.

It would be a static society—or, rather, one striving to be static, but slipping progressively out of touch with the changes taking place, unstoppably, around it and within it. And as that discrepancy increased, the efforts of the group to save itself, and its rules, by arresting change would become more rigid, more desperate, more punitive. A Grand Inquisitor would preside over the Tribunal, sentence miscreants to the pyre.

Does not all creativity originate in boundary violation, in breaking through to realms outside the old limits?

The stupid and the cautious tend to obey the rules: the stupid because they fail to recognize how easily the rules may be subverted with impunity, the cautious because they fear the group's ability to punish.

The intelligent and the bold tend to violate the rules: seeing the loopholes, the endless opportunities for evasion and concealment, and perceiving, further, how far the change-resistant rules have lagged behind a changing social reality, how benighted therefore some of these rules have come to be, still asserting, as they do, a horse-and-buggy morality in an age of superhighways, they take liberties—so easily they may not even notice.

The completely moral life—that is, the meticulous observance of all of the rules—leads, for both the individual and the group, to a rigidity that falls increasingly at odds with a changing world. Yet boundary violations, if reckless—recklessness measurable, usually, only after the act and its consequences—destroy the individual and destroy the social order. The individual becomes an outlaw, the group becomes a mob.

Well, then, how much? What is the rule to guide us in the judicious breaking of rules? What is a wise measure of violation?

"Pain is not the main thing," she says, "not the worst thing. It's not even very important. Worse is to play it safe, never to risk everything for the one big thing that comes only once, that looms, for a moment only, and then is gone. Once and once only. There's just a moment when we can go for it, leap, spend it all; or be prudent, hang back, listen to the cautious voices around us, and see that one big thing disappear forever."

The one big thing, that's the issue, to go for it or not. That one big thing—"costing not less than every-thing"—big enough maybe to justify a crime, our one chance to climb up and out of meaninglessness.

Time is running out and I cannot see—but I dread—what lies beyond.

Am I really struggling toward a moral decision? Or am I scrambling for a credible begging of the question? What a fallible calculus this is, even to the most disinterested—and I am the most interested of all.

Should I then disqualify myself, put it in the hands of a wise man?

I distrust wise men.

Anyway I know I could control the outcome by knowing the leanings of the wise man in whose hands I would place it. (You see? I am a wise man myself.)

Should I leave it to God?

I don't believe in God.

There is no escape from arbitrariness. In the hands of the most interested party lies the full responsibility for a disinterested decision.

May God have mercy on those whose fate is in my hands.

Her voice is dark, liquid, mysterious. She speaks slowly, with long pauses, searching for the right emphasis, the exact inflection. Sometimes her eyes lay hold of mine with an imploring pull, as if grasping my hand, asking me to find something between the words. At times she abandons English altogether and there then pours over me a lyrical torrent, her full lips dancing on the cascading words. I watch her mouth, the glimpse of tongue. "What were you saying?" I will ask finally.

"I was telling you how much I love you. How much . . . and all the different ways . . . and since you don't understand what I'm saying I'm not shy. You'd be shocked, *amore,* and I ashamed . . . but there it is, I can't help myself."

Her skin has a faint lemony smell. My own skin tingles, the hair rises on my arms. My mind swarms with a carnality become sublime, the smooth sweet flesh, so close, so close, the wispy hair near her ear that moves with her breathing, the remorseless, unplumbed eyes.

I feel the ache of love, the unquenchable burning. It seeks union, will be satisfied by nothing less than everything. It will burn on and on within me until I am left in ashes. The only cure is the waning of love that follows upon the fusion that love so insistently demands.

Disorder rules my life. I carry on, wander through the days like a sleepwalker.

She will risk everything. Instantly, without weighing the cost. Does not need to know the cost because she would pay any price. Prudent, self-interested carefulness is foreign to her. Our love is, for her, of supreme importance; she will do whatever is necessary to keep it, to protect it.

Weeks of longing, weeks of standing at the verge, inching closer. Vertigo. Dragged by desire, trying to stay the fall.

I am trying to reason my way out of a maze of guilt and longing. Would I, I ask myself, want everybody free to commit adultery? Or nobody? Do I want the rule of fidelity abolished? Or to be binding for most of us but not for all? Not for me?

But I'm not seeking rules—for anybody. Rules! I know nothing. I'm stumbling in the dark, trying to find a way to live, knowing that anything I find will be provi-

sional, fallible, revocable, but knowing also there's nothing
else for it unless I'm willing to follow someone else's rule,
and I'm not.

Duty, faithfulness, self-restraint, all admirable traits, but
how is one to know whether abiding by them bespeaks a
free choice of the good or a conformity to the group
driven by fear? A caring for others or a quaking at the
consequences of pursuing self-interest? If we are too
frightened to be bad, we would not wish our goodness to
be recognized as issuing from cowardice, would derive it
rather from love, courage, honor.

One promises fidelity to a spouse. Is it ever justified to
violate that promise? When? In what circumstances? Or
should one ask, rather, is it ever justified, over the course
of a lifetime, *never* to violate that promise?

Moral rules are the tools the holders of power use to
extend their power and subjugate everybody else; and the
moral man defends, unwittingly, by way of his morality,
the existing social order with its accrued and always
increasing evils.

Creative change in a society issues from violations great
enough to alter the social structure, but not so great as to
bring it down altogether. One wants a society of law that

allows some laws to be ignored. It is those violations we let stand that organize the ongoing transformation of social structure.

In 1950 contraception was still illegal in Massachusetts. Condoms labeled *For Use in the Prevention of Disease* could be sold: disease prevention was not against the rules, and the rule-enforcers could affect ignorance of the fact that most of those condoms were used to prevent pregnancy. But condoms spoil the fun, diaphragms are better; so the housewives of Massachusetts would drop off their kids at school and drive down to New Haven, where a physician could, without risk of arrest, fit them with diaphragms—thereby both breaking the law and heralding a new order. And the fact that Massachusetts law-enforcement agencies turned a blind eye enabled a change that was anyway unstoppable to come about without burnings at the stake.

The observance of rules, with a wise measure of slippage, coupled with the violation of rules, with an ironic measure of prudence, creates flexibility, strengthens the group, and thereby creates the possibility of nonviolent change in the social order.

The luxury cruise is a bore but not an escape. Too much blue hair, too much high-pitched cackle straining for the lilt of youth. The knifelike prow cuts through the dark water like a plow crossing an endless plain. A slow regular rise and fall, a steady furled-back ribbon. This furrow closes over, leaves no trace. The problem is in me, clings to me. No solution in sight.

People nearby. Promenaders. Voices are lowered as they pass close to me. I do not turn from the rail, remain fixed on the dark water. Are they concerned by my posture, my trance? Do they wonder if I meditate a leap? Do I?

Very deep here. Fathoms, fathoms, miles, the Marianas Trench, five miles of water straight down. I picture the deepening strata, the dolphin, the fish, the monsters, the leviathan, and on down. At five hundred feet the marlin, and on down where no light reaches and no life moves. Nothing. Nothing except some slimy, sightless, eyeless thing, and what sort of life is that? And on down in eternal darkness to the final black bottom and nothing there except, perhaps, the rotting timbers of ancient shipwreck and, more modern mishap, the silent hull of a submarine with its entombed now-skeleton warriors, their bony hands on the controls of now-eternally-motionless torpedoes.

The light around me fails, the water is black, a phosphorescent edge to the endless, transient furrow. Voices recede, die away. Nothing now but the rush of wind and water. Without looking I know myself to be alone. No one would hear the splash. Or the cry. How cold would it be? How long would I last? When would I be missed?

Why do I imagine this? What am I doing with these

images? What is real? Am I watching flickering shadows on the wall of a cave? Are joys and sorrows but electrical currents in a network of brain cells? Is love real?

The water. This dark water. That's real. And what is water? Something cold, wet, the embrace of death, the downward pull, the choking, the bursting lungs.

But someone else, some ghostlike other, standing beside me, looking down, seeing what I see, might say: "It's molecules of H_2O; that's what it *really* is." And if his interest were its chemistry, its boiling point, its dissolved salts, he would be right. And still different would be its reality for a swimmer, or for a marine biologist. My interest is life-weary. Lovesick, lovesick.

There is no real reality. The real from one perspective is illusion from another. Reality is made, not given. Atoms are no more final than fish, and melancholy yearning is as real as those sightless monsters in the remote depths below me.

What can two people do in one room? I look around me at the elegant emptiness. Teak parquet floor, a stately ebony piano asserting a dignity and certainty I cannot find in my own life, carpets from Persia, Bukhara, the Caucasus, Shiraz, Durbend, Turkoman, on the wall a Tekke, color of old blood, intricate geometric patterns skewed here and there by the errors and improvisations of the distracted, hungry, and perhaps—who knows?—

lovesick nomads clustered about their desert tents on those high, wind-racked Kirghiz steppes. Where are they now, those sad faces staring out of that wasteland? What has become of *their* reality, whatever it was?

Once. Only once, and never again. The recurring comforts us, she said; the singular breaks our hearts, must not be missed.

What can a man and a woman do in one room?

Well, many things, to be sure, from love to murder, but can they with their frail hands, their oh-so-suggestible minds, their vulnerable hearts, create something eternal? Can they shape a variant reality beyond the onrushing transience, hold it safe against the weight that leans against these walls, the massive onslaughts to come? Can they make their glittering transcendence *last*?

One day all this will be only memory. We will look back, she and I, to find garden or gulf, forest or desert, immutable contours then, now being shaped out of will and desire and fear, of thinnest air and hazardous dream; and whether that then-unalterable landscape proves to have been vaporous fantasy or true love will follow upon the leap we now do or do not make.

Sometimes it seems that all my analyzing, which aims to control experience, is but a shadow play on the surface of

experience. It controls nothing, it but measures my
demand that experience be understandable. Life trips me,
I am in a maze, every day a new mystery. I wrap interpretations around the peculiar shapes that impact on me, try
to subjugate them, reduce them to order. I *clothe* experience. Presented with a hunchback, I can, good tailor that
I am, cut a coat to fit, but my coats correct no deformi-
ties, nor tell me anything of the peculiar shape of the next
customer I shall have to deal with.

How to live?
    Who knows the question knows not how.
    Who knows not the question cannot tell.

Who knows the question lives in conflict, makes choices,
sees that each choice obliterates its opposite, and has
learned that the needs of the individual and the needs of
others contend and intersect in ways so complex and
confusing that no sure answer is possible.

    Who knows not the question is mute. The birds in
flight cannot instruct us, nor the shy deer, nor the cobra
poised to strike. They know how, know so unreflectively
they cannot tell. We can't go back.

    Those who live for themselves alone, unburdened by
the needs and rights of others, observing the rules only to
the degree required to stay out of jail, always in a running

skirmish with the group but never in conflict within themselves, *they* know how, know without ever having known the question: Fuck you, buddy! I've got mine, now you get yours.

But the question that cannot be answered cannot, either, be shelved. We cannot stop living until we have learned how. The train is moving. No itinerary, no briefing, no classes for beginners. We're on our way. Our first improvisation is our one chance to do it right.

VIII

Loss

So we had our season in heaven, we were not cheated. Heaven is never more than a glance and it's gone. We wanted it to last forever. We made promises.

Our lives are operatic. However poorly we sing, we are faithful to our one refrain: love, betrayal, revenge. We can't settle on love alone, the other two are equally and inalienably our nature. The most we can hope for is to love a lot and go light on the other two.

"It doesn't mean anything," she said, referring to a fling while I was away. She looks at me tenderly. "Are you okay about this? It doesn't mean anything, you know."

She's right. A roll in the hay, a sport and a pastime, it doesn't mean anything.

"I had to tell you," she says. "I couldn't just not tell you."

I examine her face, the mysterious brown eyes with curving lashes and black brows, the playful smile, the elegant sensual mouth—that mouth! I realize with a shock, that henceforth forever I will be driven to see as one that has sucked another man's cock! And is unchanged! Yet is totally changed! I'm going mad! That exquisite mouth on which my lips linger at night, lovingly, breathing in her breath as it comes from deep inside her, that mouth! unchanged yet gone forever; and I realize also, with a deep and mournful wonderment, that should I undress her and open her legs and examine her most intimate and hidden places, I would—however bright the illumination, however diligent the search—find no trace of the use to which they have been put. She is unchanged, the damage is all within me.

Once we undertook something really splendid, she and I. For love we took up arms against transience. "It means everything," she had said, "or it means nothing." "You will have me," she had promised, "for as long as you live." This splendid project had long been a shambles; but the failure, which, like a palace in ruins, still was grand and had some dignity, is now trivialized. What's left is a very little thing, and what still is possible for us is not very much, nothing that might call for passion or anguish or hope.

She observes my troubled expression, kisses me. "It doesn't mean anything!" she says again.

But it does! The pain in my heart is the meaning. And what does that pain say? *Nothing stays.*

Lips and legs and lingerie, and laughter in the night, all swirling into the void. And temples, palaces, and pyramids, and stone heroes on stone horses. And continents that split apart and drift, and stars that collapse and implode, and we are a flicker of desire in a torrent of fire and ice, and she's right, it doesn't mean anything, it all slides away, going, going, going.

Once our love had been so strong that it claimed sexuality as its own, subjugated it to its own spiritual purposes, making of the union of bodies the supreme expression of love. That regency had fallen, and sex without the embrace of love had become common, and love without the energy of lust had become weightless.

I was stricken with loss, but knew it was no accident, that it was in the nature of things, that some promises have to be broken, that Heaven is a whistle stop, not a destination, that exalted love can never last, always falls to dailiness; and also that the yearning that it be eternal is ineluctable, and beyond consolation—except that out of the defeat sometimes something of beauty can be made. And I realized also that in some way I had always known this, that it was stated unmistakably in the music I most loved, in the Schubert Notturno in E-flat, the last movement of the Mahler Fourth, the slow middle section of the Chopin Polonaise in F-sharp Minor.

I must not yearn. I have not been cheated. Honeydew has wet my lips, I have heard the sea girls sing, I have drunk the milk of paradise. I've had it—gloriously!—one way; now I have it the other. It has got to be all right either way.

Memories spring up around me like prison walls, images swarm and sting like hornets: her nakedness, the postures of surrender, of vulnerability, the voluntary, somewhat anxious defenselessness, the wide frightened eyes, then the trust, the melting, the giving of it all, "Take me, I'm yours!"

I had a treasure, but somehow I lost it; or, perhaps, I had an ordinary thing but somehow mistook it for a treasure. In our sorrow is this not the choice we ponder? To which we must find an answer? And does not the answer we find tell us who we are? We the believers, and those others who know that the treasure of love is always a mirage, who therefore never seek it, never find it, would not recognize it if it fell in their lap, and who, never having known the transcendence, never know the fall, never know this sorrow.

I am a believer, who knows that all meaning is illusion, yet am driven ceaselessly to seek it, achieving thereby the worst of both worlds, retaining neither the stoicism of the one who stands unmoving in the blistering desert, nor the hope of the one who stumbles on after the shimmering blue water.

We affirm a continuing deathless passion, but it is not the same. It has lost its wildness and voracity, has become a passion remembered, a passion respected, a passion manqué.

There can be no contract in loving. What comes is a blessing, one is not entitled to it, can lay no claim when it is lost, one gives as one can.

Maybe the right way to fall in love is to accept at the outset that it won't last. Accept, not in the sense of resigning one's self to a sad inevitability, but in the sense of celebrating a process that unavoidably entails the ending of a passion that presently appears as life's supreme value.

Looking at her, I should not feel the ache of future loss, but an unmixed celebration of what I now have. I should accept change not because I cannot anyway prevent it, but because it is life itself. Love and the end of love, like life and death, must be praised as one.

The danger in striving for permanence is not that one will fail, but that one may in some stifled measure succeed, thereby preserving a fading relationship behind a mask of love that falls increasingly at variance with the withering face behind it. Yearning for permanence is failure of nerve, cowardice in face of the risks and opportunities of living.

I am as if brain-damaged. Life has distanced itself, is taking place behind a veil; and sometimes, surrounded by books, I realize I don't want to read, and, wrenched by longing, that I don't want music, and it will seem to me that I am reaching into myself for a silence beyond the absence of sound, for a stolen preview perhaps of that stillness that lies on the other side.

I am stricken with loss, also with guilt. Whom have I loved, truly? To whom have I given myself, fully, holding nothing back? Have I trusted any woman enough to stand fully exposed before her, fully vulnerable? Is it any different now? I *feel* that it's different, that I bring to her something more authentic, more worthy, but how do I know? Needing her to cover over the emptiness might very well present itself as true love.

Madison Avenue. Crowds swirl by. A tugging on my sleeve, I turn. A madman, gaunt, cloaked, forlorn, saying, "Tell me about your true love's hair." I impale him on my vacant stare, vacant because now I am looking inward, feeling my loss. "My true love's hair," I say, "is a silken fall of glimmering lights, a dark wood with glints of autumn, coffee and cherry and chocolate brown, and fallen leaves all around." "May God have mercy on your soul," the madman says, and vanishes in the crowd.

IX

Love

Falling in love is a madness. No treatment is required, indeed none is effective. It is self-limited in time, recovery is certain and spontaneous. In the aftermath, however, one may find oneself joined for life to a partner one would not in any normal state have chosen.

The disorder generally runs a benign course. But it *is* a madness. One loses contact with reality, clutches jealously to one's breast something one believes to be a treasure while everyone else sees plainly it is but an ordinary loaf of bread.

The opportunity to love is ever-present. No one, in his loneliness, need ever say, "I wish I had someone to love." That someone is right there. The trouble is she has become real, while only the still-imaginary inspires us to love.

We say we want love, and surely we do, but we want it to flow toward us, a great wave splashing over us, bountifully; we are not so eager that it flow outward, away from us to others who might need it more than we.

We live by attachment, not by reason. There is no value without caring, and caring is loving. That's the point: one's own life has value only because one cares for others. And one cares *without a reason*! Without reflection, without the weighing of profit and loss. The caring that justifies everything else is itself without justification. It is a leap.

Attachments grow in the dark, like roots. Silently, invisibly, they extend themselves in heart-soil, anchoring us in the world. To go on living then is not elective; we cannot depart this life, we are held by invincible tendrils.

After arriving at the peak of sexual desirability we begin a long process of decline. Imperceptible for a few years,

but then beyond overlooking. We are becoming less lovable. There's no stopping it short of dying young. And if
we live long enough—proceed far enough into ugliness
and decay—we are not lovable at all. Whatever attention
still comes our way flows from duty, however well camouflaged as caring.

Concurrently, as we grow older, we become less and
less able to love others, and if we live long enough we
become incapable of loving at all, our concern reaching
then no further than our pains and malfunctions. Irrita-
bly aware of the diminishment of love coming toward
us, we tend not to notice that we, equally, are giving less
to others.

To grow old gracefully one must accept, without protest
or dismay, the diminishment of incoming love. More, one
must *anticipate* it, always positioning oneself to receive less
than that which is voluntarily offered.

Never ask or plead or sue for love. The time for wooing is over, this is the time for farewell.

Two things I know for sure about love: no one ever gets
enough, and you can't get more by asking. To the beggar
for money a few real coins may fall, but the beggar for
love is a fool. Into his upturned hat, along with the
humiliation, will fall only scraps of guilt and duty falsely

labeled as love. The only way to get more love is to give more love.

Beware! Wooing may be hidden. Too much giving, too much attentiveness, too many presents, may be but the mask for asking. You've had your turn; now get out of the way. Make room for others.

Who can map the vast terrain of love? The sublime heights, the dismal swamps. There are no certified experts, anyone may try his hand. What do *I* know about love? What varieties have fallen to me? What has been meant when a woman has said to me, I love you?

What if she whispers it, at night? What if she *breathes* it in my ear, our arms tightening around each other, her legs parting? "I love you," she says. What does it mean?

"I want to take you in my mouth, in my arms, every night, want it so much I hallucinate it, your body hard and bony against mine, mine a yielding softness against yours. I want to feel you knocking at the door, and I want you to feel how utterly I welcome you, draw you in, make you part of myself. I want our mouths to become one mouth, want us to breathe together, the breath filling your depths at one moment, in the next filling mine. We become more than ourselves—and less—the future and the past disappear, the present is all, is swollen with all future and all past. Sex becomes then something sacred and dangerous, perhaps blasphemous, mysterious and holy. Tenderness will embrace passion, and passion exalt love, and for a moment—which may devour all eternity—we will become a pillar of dazzling light, timeless, mindless, complete. We may never come back."

This is the pinnacle, the very Matterhorn of love, but the air is thin and it's slippery underfoot. One can't stay there long.

What if we are alone together in the kitchen? Night has fallen In all the dark house only this one room is lighted. Beyond the house, the vast forest. She is standing at the stove, serving. Now she places the two plates of food before us. She removes her apron, sits, spreads her napkin, raises her eyes to mine in a calm level gaze. Suddenly her face softens, a wave of emotion sweeps over her. Impulsively, she reaches out her hand, places it on mine. "I love you," she says. What does it mean?

"I'm so lucky to have you! I cherish you, I would be lost without you. I'm so glad we are moving through life like this, together, our lives everywhere commingled, inseparable. You are not *at* the center of my life, you *are* the center of my life."

I've been here five days, my visit is over. Perhaps I have stayed too long. I stand up—with some difficulty, my arthritis is getting worse. We embrace. The woman in my arms is my daughter, forty-five years old. Her lips are at my ear: "I love you," she says.

Only on farewell, our faces hidden from each other by the embrace, does she say it. I understand: face to face, looking in my eyes, it would veer too close to that buried erotic tie which, we agree, must remain buried. "I love you," she says. What does it mean?

"I care for you. You are dear to me. I grew up in the shelter of your protective love. I'm grateful to you for so many things. I want you to be well, to be happy. I want you to live a long time. I will look after you, safeguard you, be responsible for you."

I am propped up in bed in the nursing home. I still have two or three friends, but they are old, too, and can't get about much. I am waiting impatiently for my daughter's weekly visit. Why doesn't she come? Why is she always late? She arrives, kisses me on the forehead, runs her fingers through my lingering hair. She has brought presents:

a box of candy, a CD of Maria Callas, a TV no larger than my hand. I complain to her about the food, about my heartburn, my incontinence, the indifferent nurses. She will speak to the director about it. She pushes me about the grounds in my wheelchair. The visit is over. But she has only just arrived! Why won't she stay? Why does she always rush away? She stands at the door, jaunty and cheerful, blows a kiss with her fingertips. "I love you," she says. What does it mean?

"Poor thing. Everything falling apart. But still dear to me. So much to remember. I will look after him—with reluctance (already I feel it), and eventually (I'm afraid) with irritable impatience. But he's my father. I will take care of him."

Conscientious cartographer that I am, I must sketch for you a small bleak place lying just beyond the domain of love. Contiguous, but unmistakably beyond.

I sit in a wheelchair before a large box with a glistening bright surface. I don't know what it is. I don't like it. Figures move senselessly about the screen, shout, laugh, grimace, talk unintelligibly. Other people, also in wheelchairs, are clustered about. But we are not watching the bright box, we're staring, staring, with empty eyes, emptiness within.

Who is this woman touching my arm? What does she

want of me? What is she saying? I don't understand. I don't trust her. Why is she looking at me like that? I will report her to the authorities.

She stays for a few minutes, then leaves.

In this place no one says, "I love you."

I live in the intermediate reaches of love. Not the best place, but certainly not the worst. I should count myself fortunate. Be alert. Love is where you find it. Don't be blinded by your categories. Love comes unexpectedly in many forms.

My daughter has given me a fountain pen. Quite beautiful and rare. A paper-thin shell of russet marble, the ink flows from the gold nib as a blue velvet ribbon unspooling itself on the white page before me. Not my birthday, no occasion, a spontaneous gift of love. She knows my fetishistic addiction to elegant writing instruments. I feel blessed, it's a good omen, may prove an inspiration, life has not yet closed in on me. Maybe I still can write something beautiful.

We arrive, my wife and I, at the Nassau Inn in Princeton for a three-day stay. My wife will be attending psychoanalytic meetings, and I will sit in our room and write with my new pen, my love pen.

We are assigned a dark and gloomy room, the inn is

full, it's all they have, tomorrow they will move us to something better. The next morning we pack our things, proceed to breakfast, and afterward go to our new room. All of our things have been carefully moved, clothes hanging decorously in the closet. Sunshine streams through large windows, outside the top branches of a sycamore tree breaking into bloom, a large comfortable chair. Wonderful!

My wife goes to her meeting, I settle down to write. Where is my pen? I search through my clothes. Haste, foreboding, fear. I ransack my briefcase, dive into the pockets on all of my clothes. Wait. Wait. Don't panic. Sit down. Think. Last night . . . ah, yes . . . I was writing in bed, I must have left it in the drawer of the bedside table. I race through the corridors to the old room. It's locked. I race through more corridors to find a maid. She understands, lets me in. I lunge for the bedside table, yank open the drawer. It's not there. The room has been "made," everything is in order, ready for the new tenant. I interview the maid who cleaned the room; she did not see my pen. I interview, one by one, all of the maids who work on the floor. Did you enter that room? Did you see my pen? None of them speak English, but they understand, they see my plight, I show them with the movements of writing, they know what I have lost. They shake their heads sadly. I call the front desk, the Lost and Found. Nothing avails, all avenues have been searched. By my carelessness I have lost what now becomes a magic wand that could have lifted me up out of dung and death. No one to blame but myself. I am the sole agent of my ruin.

I sit in the comfortable chair, in the beautiful room of light and sunshine . . . and am desolate. Hours pass. I stare at the wall. Occasionally one of the maids knocks on the door and my heart leaps with hope, but she only wants to ask if I have found it yet. Morning passes to afternoon, the light changes. I'm not hungry, I can't read. A bad omen, I feel a deep gloom.

Another knock on the door. This time it is a tiny Oriental woman, the top of her head no higher than my belt, ancient and wrinkled and wizened, speaking to me eagerly, a torrent of words, not one of which I understand. Another maid, I know from her uniform. I feel her goodwill, but shake my head sadly. No, I tell her, I haven't found it. She perseveres, will not give up. The communication impasse is total. Words do not avail. I start to close the door. She pulls on my sleeve with her tiny, clawlike fingers, beckons urgently, races away, looks back, sees that I am not following, comes back, beckons more urgently. She is agitated, I am loath to follow. What does she want of me? She races away down the long corridor like a deer, turning, looking back over her shoulder, beckoning, becoming more and more girlish as she runs, the wizened years falling away, and I am caught up by her energy and hope, and I do follow, and she races on even faster now that she knows I am following, and after many corridors and many turns we arrive at a closet and she flings open that door, reaches in, and brings forth . . . my pen! And instantly sees in my face that yes, yes, this is it, the very one; and I feel so blessed, and she so ethereally happy at having been able to help me, and I look down on this tiny frail ancient person, with her happy wrinkled face, and realize that her tugging on my sleeve, her not giving up, her racing down the corridor—that, too, is love.

ACKNOWLEDGMENTS

The author acknowledges his indebtedness, for passages concerning Hitler and Nazi Germany, to John Toland, *Adolf Hitler* (New York: Doubleday & Company, Inc., 1976); for comments about crowds and for the description of a Stone Age hunting pack, to Elias Canetti, *Crowds and Power* (New York: Continuum, 1978). The statement of President McKinley is quoted by Reinhold Niebuhr, *Moral Man and Immoral Society* (New York: Charles Scribner's Sons, 1932).